PERMANENT HAPPINESS

The Only Way to Find Peace, Joy, and Your Life-Given Purpose

D1369672

Iyabo Ojikutu, MD

Formatting by Rik – Wild Seas Formatting

First Printing, 2017

ISBN: 978-0-692-88489-8

ISBN: 0-692-88489-0

Dr. Iyabo's Books and More Inc.

Atlanta, GA

iyaboojikutu.com

Dedication

This book is dedicated to the precious spirit of my dad, who passed away two months before I started writing this book. He died at the ripe age of eighty-six on October 14, 2015.

My father was the greatest dad ever, the best any child could ask for. He was a gentle, calm soul. He was my best mentor and a great influencer. I learned a great deal from him—not only from his words but from his general demeanor, his unspoken words, and his actions.

He would be so proud if he were still alive to read this book.

Daddy, may your soul continue to rest in peace. You are my hero. Here's to you…I've created "the only way" book.

Acknowledgments

My deepest thanks go to my parents for the unconditional love and nurturing they blessed me with from a very early age. Without them, this book would have never come to be.

To my lovely daughters, Reni and Moni, for being such beautiful souls and for always challenging me to be the best mother I can be.

To my editor, Elizabeth Zack Myers of BookCrafters LLC, for putting the Midas touch on my manuscript. I am deeply thankful to you for the amazing work you did with the structural editing.

To Dori Harrell, for being the best copyeditor and for your final look-through. Your phenomenal dedication to this project is one I will never forget.

Emilie Hendryx, thank you for an amazing design job. Anna Gordon Portraits, for the wonderful shots.

Finally, I would like to thank my heavenly Father for His love, grace, and mercy.

Table of Contents

Chapter 1 - Happiness and Peace   1

Chapter 2 - My Transformation   21

Chapter 3 - Be the Change Our Children Need   41

Chapter 4 - Our Relationships   61

Chapter 5 - Faith and Works   93

Chapter 6 - Our Spiritual Lives   113

Chapter 7 - Our Physical Lives   125

Chapter 8 - Light and Darkness   139

Chapter 9 - Ask for Help   151

Chapter 10 - What We Need to Live Will Follow   155

Chapter 11 - It Is All Possible   157

Find peace and joy, and live out your life-given purpose.

Chapter 1

Happiness and Peace

Peace is permanent happiness.

Happiness is good, but is not enough. Peace is good, and is enough.

When I realized the close link between our physical and spiritual lives, I felt inspired to write this book.

We are all extremely powerful spiritual beings. I discovered this once I started to live a quieter life, canceling out noise and chaos from my daily life, journaling more, and having longer prayer and reflection times. *As I lived my life in this way, I connected much more deeply with my spiritual essence.*

There are so many distractions in life. Kids, work, deadlines, relationships, and so on. (You know what I'm talking about, right?) These elements are important things in their own ways, but they run parallel to pursuing peace and finding meaning to life. Let me explain.

Imagine two straight lines that have no end until the day we depart from this world. These two lines are our *spiritual* and *physical* lines. (I will refer to them as *lines, lives,* or *lifelines* throughout this book.)

Our *spiritual lifelines* have to do with everything that affects our heart and soul issues, and our inner cores—our spirits. Our *physical lifelines* are everything that affects our bodies, the vessels that house our souls and spirits while we are still alive on this earth.

Throughout our lives we are walking in forward motion in the middle between these two lines. These parallel lines will never meet or intersect, but they do continue at the same rate as each other throughout our life spans. They are lines we have to *simultaneously* nourish in order to achieve our goals of peace and permanent happiness.

When life throws us curveballs, as it certainly does, our lines sometimes curve or bend in response to the adverse or chaotic life circumstances. But even so, the lines remain parallel to one another, and we remain in the middle of them...hopefully moving ahead in forward motion.

Without both these lines in our life, we cannot thrive. We must keep moving forward; we must continue seeking *both physically and spiritually.* For example, if you make really bad food choices, do not exercise, and get out of shape physically, and you pursue only matters of the heart and soul, your life will get out of sync. Conversely, if you abandon matters of the heart and only pursue work, deadlines, and physical activity, your life will dramatically, rapidly, and terribly fall out of sync.

We must work, meet deadlines, and take care of our physical bodies...just as we must also get in tune with heart issues, connect with our spiritual beings, and pursue peace and happiness. I have found that without permanent happiness and peace, life is meaningless.

Yet we can only really realize our spiritual essences *when we start to be still and quiet more often so that we can better connect with our spirits.* The reality is, most people are in touch with their physical lives but not with—or to a much lesser degree—their spiritual lives, so they never begin or experience the process of pursuing peace.

My goal and hope is to help my readers understand why we are here in this universe and how to live a meaningful life as we pass through it. We all can agree that we are passing through this life. None of us will be here forever physically. Our physical lives will depart from this world sooner or later. But guess what? *Our spirits live on*...hence the importance of really knowing how to pursue matters of the heart. We want our spirits to live on in the supernatural realm, even when we are no longer present physically, and to help others who are still housing their spirits in their physical bodies here on earth.

Permanent Happiness is not a book that will make you perfect, wealthy, or more beautiful or accomplished. What it will do, however, is help you navigate through all aspects of life, and find peace, hope, and comfort in every situation and life circumstance you encounter, whether positive or adverse. This will go a long way toward making you a full, complete person whose life has true meaning.

I do have a special hope too for our teens and youth—to really tune in closely to this book so they may start to understand how to live out their given purposes. If they start nourishing their two lifelines at an early age, this will influence their life growth into adulthood more than if they understand this truth only when they are older.

Why This "One" Book

There are many, many good books out there on diet and exercise, relationships, career, prosperity, money management, coping with sickness and the loss of loved ones, religion, peace, and spirituality. I have read many of them, and several have inspired and influenced me positively. However, never could I find a book that put all the fundamentals and necessities of life under one cover!

I *craved* a single volume that I could read over and over again to help me find balance in both my spiritual life and my physical life. I wanted it to be a book I could refer to for *all* of life's circumstances. At the same time, it needed to be easy to relate to, connect with, and understand. It had to help people realize the importance of both their spiritual and physical lives being parallel lines flanking them through their lifetimes. It had to be a title that did not have too many complex medical terms or scientific studies, making it difficult for the average person to follow and understand. Too, I wanted it to be something readers could place in their purses or on their nightstands so they could easily access it for answers on how to make sense of any life circumstances they were experiencing, or, in fact, *not* experiencing.

I wrote this book to fill that void so that the world would no longer lack a single book teaching us how to bring our spiritual and physical lives together in detail.

A Message, a Gift

I have always been an optimist. I have always believed in the concept of hard work, hope, perseverance, and possibility. Also, I am very determined. I'm not exactly sure where I got each of these traits from, but I have had them from early childhood on. I would like to believe my parents passed them on to me by way of genetics and by the example they lived out.

My parents never told me directly that I must have hope or that all things are possible if I truly believe and work hard for them. However, one thing I constantly heard about from them was the value of education: "Iyabo, you must study hard; you must pass your exams. Education is very important." Those words still echo in my mind, even now. At forty-five years old (as of this writing), I can still hear their words buzzing in my brain, for they are words of possibility and truth.

My dad had started to pass on this truth to my daughters, Reni and Moni, right before he died. In fact, they were his last words to my youngest daughter, Moni, on the last day we saw him—waiting to check my parents in at the airport for the flight back to their home in Lagos, Nigeria.

In the Atlanta airport, my father sat down with my daughter Moni (age eleven at the time) to give her a ten-minute talk on the importance of education. Hopefully, she will pass his words of wisdom on to her own children, and they to their children, from generation to generation.

What a great message I have echoing in my soul—and now in my daughters' souls, passed on to them from their grandfather. *Get an education, and get a good life.* These are very true words…and words have tremendous power and influence on us.

I believe God gave this message to me as a gift. It is a gift that I appreciate so much, and I am trying to pass on what I have learned about life, God, and the value of education through this book.

Who I Am

I have always worked hard for everything I have done and achieved in life, doing so with the firm belief that my attempts would be successful and would come through exactly as I hoped. I would much rather live life as an optimist than a pessimist. I am, however, also a realist; I don't elevate myself too much beyond my possibilities. I don't strive toward an unrealistic point and thus set myself up for failure. So I am realistic.

That written, I am also a dreamer. And I always dream big. I dream about what I would like to see happen in my life; first visualizing it in great detail and then going out and working toward achieving it just as visualized. What helps me along the way is my trait of perseverance: I have never been a quitter. I keep going for something, keeping my eye on the goal, researching what efforts and resources need to be poured in for success to happen, and staying the course until I achieve my goal. This is something each and every one of us has the power to do.

But if I am completely transparent…I have quit once in my life. And as you read on, you will find out what I ended up quitting. I had no choice, and I had to quit the very thing that I had tried for so long to hold on to. It was a life element into which I had poured my heart, soul, time, resources, and trust. And this may come as a surprise, but it was my optimistic outlook that actually enabled and empowered me to quit this thing. Yes, that's right: *the optimist in me asked me to quit.*

An optimist? And also a quitter? Doesn't that sound like two people who are opposites or who hold two opposite qualities? A lot of you must be thinking, *Optimists should not be quitters!* Well, sometimes optimists *do* quit because their souls are telling them there is better and there is more, and they can only experience "better" and "more" if they "let go and let in."

Being both an optimist and a quitter worked out in my favor at the time. You see, I knew and believed life had to be better than it was at that precise moment. I recognized my life was not meant to continue down the same path and that I had no peace around the situation I was in. This realization meant I had to *break free* to get my lines back to straight (they were curved at the time) and return to my journey of pursuing peace and permanent happiness.

Lessons, not Failures

Optimists do not look at situations that do not work out as failures. They look at them as *lessons*. In every failing or unsuccessful situation there is always something to *learn, run with,* and *use for a greater purpose.*

So it is okay to sometimes quit specific situations. If you do not quit a situation or circumstance that is failing, you cannot embark on a subsequent succeeding situation. That failing circumstance will hold you in perfect bondage unless you let go of it or find a perfect solution to turn it around. It is impossible to move ahead if you are holding on to a negative situation. (I will discuss this further in the book.)

So who I am, generally speaking, is a realistic and optimistic non-quitting dreamer. All of us must have a combination of all these qualities (realism, optimism, and steadfastness) in order to live a life aimed at meeting our life goals as we pursue peace and happiness.

Powerful Peace

Why do I start with mentioning peace?

Peace is a word that we use loosely without fully understanding its strength and meaning. It is a very powerful word. *Peace* encompasses all the components of the fruit of the spirit: love, joy, patience, kindness, goodness, faithfulness, gentleness, and self-control—and peace itself (Gal. 5:22).

Peace, then, is the pursuit to embrace and live by the fruit of the spirit intuitively in our everyday interactions with others and ourselves. And this pursuit of peace is the main element in living in a state of permanent happiness.

The aforementioned sentiment is from the Bible, Galatians 5:22, but bear with me: I'm not planning on quoting the Bible throughout this book. This is not a "religious" book, and it is not meant for any specific religious groups or factions. It is a book for *all* mankind.

My goal here through the usage of Galatians 5:22 is merely to point out what the *fruit of the spirit* is. The fruit of the spirit are heart issues and issues fundamental to living out a meaningful and peaceful life. Rather than "religious" words, they are words of truth that apply to *every living being* in this world. (Thanks for hanging in there with me!)

Now, if you choose to live by Galatians 5:22 and embody the fruit of the spirit in your daily life, you are on your way to pursuing peace. But it may surprise you to discover you don't have to embody every component of the fruit of the spirit to get closer to peace!

Why would that be? *Because no component of the fruit of the spirit can exist all by itself!* Think about it: Have you ever met a kind person who is not honest? I haven't yet, and I don't think I ever will. It is almost impossible to be kind without being honest. Have you met a person who has pure love for others but is not gentle in spirit? Nope. How about a person who has a grateful heart but is not patient? Nope.

The qualities all naturally coexist with each other! **You only need to consciously pick one to work on, and once you put it into practice, then the others are subconsciously added on to you.** How beautiful and powerful that is! Practice one…get the benefits of the others! How rewarding, effortless, and sweet it is.

So once you start choosing to be kind to others, you will be patient and honest and have a grateful heart. Or, once you start to have a grateful heart, you will have no choice but to love purely and be patient and kind…and this fills you with joy.

Can you have pure love for someone else and not be patient? No, impossible. Loving others purely means learning to see their points of view, getting to know them, listening to them, being there for them, and being nonjudgmental. This requires patience and self-control.

It is so easy to immerse ourselves in the pursuit of peace, since all we have to do is just choose to live by *one* of the fruit of the spirit—and the others come along automatically!

What a simple concept, but ever so powerful. Let's explore it a bit more by turning it into a practical exercise for at home, at work, or wherever you are!

Put It into Practice

I'm going to pick "kindness": I want you to choose to have a kind heart toward others and to practice this for thirty days. What would this look like in everyday life?

You should choose to be kind to and thank everyone with whom you come into contact: your parents, mentors, teachers, grocery store clerk, your boss, the cleaner or janitor at your child's school, your employees, your grandparents, your kids, your neighbors, and your friends. Do this for thirty days. Smile genuinely, hold the door, help an elderly neighbor, reach out to a friend who may need your help. That's not all that hard, right? And if maybe you feel someone hasn't done anything special for you during a particular encounter, just be kind to them and thank that person for being in your life. After all, at the end of the day, no one is meant to be alone. You have these people in your life for a reason, and you also cannot exist without human interactions. If, for one moment, you think you can exist by yourself, let me assure you that you cannot. So just thank these individuals for being in your life if you can't think of anything they've done for you.

If you do this, I promise you that love, joy, peace, gentleness, patience, honesty, kindness, faithfulness, and self-control will tag right along! You'll notice at the end of the thirty days that you've been transformed. (Actually, you'll notice this after only a few days. You won't have to wait for thirty days to pass). You will have entered into that wished-for process that so many of us spend a lifetime seeking: the process of pursuing peace.

All these fruit of the spirit, including peace itself, lead us to experiencing even *more* peace.

Understanding Peace

I took care to explain peace earlier because there are various definitions of peace out there. Here are just a few of them:

- state of tranquility or quiet

- freedom from disquieting or oppressive thoughts

- pact or agreement to end hostilities between those who have been at war or in a state of enmity

- harmony in personal relations

- the normal, non-warring condition of a nation, group of nations, or the world

- interjection asking for silence or calm, or a greeting for farewell

All these definitions are comforting and should bring smiles to our faces. They spark curiosity, inspiring us to ask questions on how to achieve and sustain the state they describe. After all, peace is a state that feels really good. A state that makes us feel warm inside and brings joy.

The last definition from the preceding list is especially interesting: so many people easily utter the word "peace" as a greeting or farewell and even signal the peace sign with their hands, but they still do not understand the true meaning of the word or realize its power. What a waste of a word!

Imagine the good, positive, and powerful impact it would create in our world if we all knew the power of this word many of us have used so loosely over time. Imagine if we were actually *actively helping* people and ourselves live a life of peace as we uttered the word "peace" or made the hand sign!

Without actively pursuing peace, none of us are living a meaningful life. It is impossible. However, I can confidently say that each one of us has that one common goal: *to live a meaningful life.* Some of us may not want to admit it outright because of arrogance or self-righteousness or lack of awareness, but if we dig deep in our souls, we discover we are all yearning for lasting peace.

Unfortunately, some people spend a lifetime trying to figure out the process of pursuing peace and sadly depart from this world without ever experiencing peace. **Don't let this be you!**

The Continuum

These are the three simple steps to finding lasting peace in our lives:

1. Live by the fruit of the spirit, and be of good character.
2. Nourish our physical and spiritual lifelines.
3. Live out our life-given purposes by using our God-given gifts to magnificence and influence.

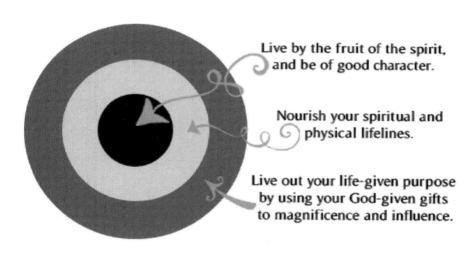

Live by the fruit of the spirit, and be of good character.

Nourish your spiritual and physical lifelines.

Live out your life-given purpose by using your God-given gifts to magnificence and influence.

It sounds so simple, yet many of us have struggled (and keep struggling) with those simple-sounding phrases. What many of us fail to comprehend is that the three steps are a continuum. We have to be working on all three steps *simultaneously* in order to continue to experience peace in our lives.

If you are influencing people and not nourishing your spiritual life, you will not have lasting peace.

If you are being kind, loving, and forgiving, yet not taking care of your physical body, your state of peace will wax and wane.

If you are taking care of your physical body and not spending time connecting with your spirit or living by the fruit of the spirit, your peace will not last.

Let me ask you, reader, which of these three steps are you struggling with? Which of them is preventing you from finding lasting peace and happiness?

What This Book Is Not

Please note the title of this book is not *Achieving Permanent Peace*, *Achieve Permanent Peace*, or *How to Achieve Permanent Peace*. That's because we cannot "achieve" or "attain" peace. We do not get to a point in our lives where we feel we have attained peace, and it will therefore stick and never depart. Nor can we sit back and "feel" the accomplishment of peace, expecting it to stay around. It does not work that way.

Peace reaches us from a continuing process of our pursuing it— pursuing all the fruit of the spirit that help us continuously experience peace—and then we keep on pursuing it. And yet again.

Why is this necessary? Well, life does get, and will get, bumpy and rocky, so if we are not actively on a pursuit of peace, we will fall, falter, and fail.

Also note, the title of this book is not *Pursue Perfection*. "Perfection" is a word I personally would like to remove from the dictionary! It has not ever been successfully defined, because it is impossible to define something that has no significance and is impossible to achieve. That means "perfect" is an unrealistic word.

Most of the definitions of "perfect" I found actually have the word "perfection" or "perfect" in them, because "perfection" just cannot be properly defined. Here are a few attempts at defining "perfection"—that is, the few I found *without* the word itself being immersed in the definition!

- The condition, state, or quality of being free or as free as possible from all flaws or defects.

- The action or process of improving something until it is

faultless or as faultless as possible.

- Something that cannot be improved.

- The highest degree of proficiency, skill, or excellence, as in some art.

- A person or thing perceived as the embodiment of perfection. (Okay, I admit this one has the word itself tucked into its definition!)

No one of us can be free from flaws and defects or be faultless or blameless. We all have something we can improve on. This means no one can have the "highest" degree of proficiency or skill. Who defines the highest skill we can have, anyway? What a subjective concept! Only the creator of the universe—God—is perfect. Of course, there are standards and scales for everything in life that we must live by as good citizens of the world, but there is no perfect person, thing, or situation. We are just as imperfect as the person about whom we are most critical.

In each of us there is some type of flaw. We should strive to be wholesome instead of wasting our time trying to be perfect. So again, this book is not about pursuing perfection.

This book is about…pursuing permanent happiness/peace. And thus it is "the only way" book, or the only way to living the life you really want to live and the life the creator of the universe intended for you to live.

The Only Way!

When I became inspired to write this book, I had come to realize (for several reasons) that the only way to get the most out of life, gain permanent happiness, and fulfill my purpose is *to bridge the gap between the physical world and the spiritual world.* That requires that we pursue peace. For if we do not pursue peace, we will not be in tune with our spirit, we will not perceive what our spirit is telling us, and we'll never be able to fulfill our life purpose.

We are all spirits living in physical bodies—although this does not mean we have to be perfect or religious. We are not required to memorize the Bible or another holy book or to be free from mistakes or sin. However, as we pursue peace and feel the benefits of our pursuit on ourselves and others around us, it motivates us to pursue it even more until the seeking eventually becomes effortless and just a part of our daily living. Through the process, we will pass the desire and inspiration on to many other people, many of whom will then start undergoing the process, making our universe a better place.

The process of pursuing peace is going on in major ways in our world right at this very moment and at quite a rapid speed. Most of us know and understand what peace is, and we want it for ourselves, either consciously or subconsciously. We try to seek it out because we crave it. But there is a problem, and it's a huge one: our process gets interrupted too often. Way too often, unfortunately.

Wanting to Be Happy

We are all aware that we want to be happy. Most human beings will agree on this. After all, how many times have you, or another, expressed the wish, "I just want to be happy!"?

Well, it is okay to wish for happiness! Happiness is *great.* The problem is, we usually associate happiness with the occurrence of positive events and situations in our lives, basing our happiness on the state of our material possessions, romantic relationships, physical health, and heart-fluttering situations (to name just a few).

Well, what happens when life isn't always that "bed of roses" we hope for? The events and situations I've just mentioned wax and wane throughout our lives. So the happiness we derive from them often involves short-lived euphoric states.

Consider this: What happens when our circumstances or situations are in positive states—but then they turn into negative situations? For example, what happens when we lose all or some possessions from the loss of a job? Or get sick, lose a loved one, or experience a breakup with a romantic partner? Our happiness is short lived and gets swept away once the negative times show up—and they will show up for sure!

For example: This morning I got a bouquet of flowers from a loved one. It made me feel special, loved, and happy. In the afternoon I went for a routine health check and received a clean bill of health from my doctor. Now I am quite happy and full of euphoria. But when bedtime came, I stayed up all night tossing and turning, worrying and anxious about the bills I had to pay and my ability to do just that. *How can this be? I just had two happy-inducing incidents earlier in the day, yet now, just a few hours later, I am not happy enough to close my eyes and sleep peacefully!*

Situation-based states that cause temporary euphoria are not our answer to everything, *for they are not sustainable.* When we link our happiness to a singular event or a cluster of singular events—and these events or situations are usually external influences—then our happiness is not sustainable.

When *is* it sustainable? When we are **pursuing peace!**

You cannot be *permanently* happy if you are not *actively* pursuing peace. For example, you could be happy today, or for a few weeks, because you just landed that new job and are finally getting a paycheck or because you met a really nice guy or girl who is now your partner. However, once that new situation becomes "the norm" in your life, don't you crave more?

"What's next for me?" you ask yourself. "I was really happy, and actually I am still doing okay because I now have that paycheck to pay my bills, and I am in love with my new partner—but I don't have deep-seated permanent happiness or joy. *How can I get that?* I was happy just the other day, but I don't feel as happy this week! Why is that?"

Well, this is because you haven't figured out a way to continuously pursue peace and experience its benefits. The key word here is *continuously.* Meaning, regardless of what life is bringing your way or throwing at you at any point, you are permanently happy.

Another way I define *peace* is as the *sustenance of happiness through the positive and negative situations in our lives.* Peace requires an active process: We have to internally choose to embark upon a quest for it for ourselves, and so it is linked to our internal beings and our personal choices. Since it is a process, it can be, and is, sustainable, and thus it can make us continuously and *permanently* happy.

My goal with this book is to **reduce those interruptions to our happiness that we all have as we embark on the process of finding *permanent happiness*, which is also known to me as...*peace*.** Yes, that's right: With and through this book, I am personally defining *peace* as *permanent happiness*. ***Peace* is a state of *PERMANENT* happiness...not just happiness!** And the only way to *be permanently* happy is by continuously pursuing peace:

1. Choosing to live by the fruit of the spirit—love, joy, peace, patience, self-control, goodness, kindness, gentleness, and faithfulness in all life circumstances (basically, consciously and internally changing our characters).

2. Continuously nourishing our physical and spiritual lifelines.

3. Using our gifts to positively influence and elevate ourselves and others.

Live by the fruit of the spirit, and be of good character.

Nourish your spiritual and physical lifelines.

Live out your life-given purpose by using your God-given gifts to magnificence and influence.

Notice how these involve internal strength and power. We are actively and consciously making choices to **enter and remain in that process of continually pursuing peace, regardless of all life's circumstances.**

Yes, happiness is good, but it is not enough. Peace is good, and it *is* enough.

Sticking with It

There are so many distractions in life that keep interrupting our pursuit of peace and true fulfillment process. My hope is to help my readers reduce them to a point where everyone "gets it" and gets on board with the process…and the effects are ginormous. *Does that word even exist?* Yes, it does! It is a word. (I did check.)

Remember, I'm an optimist, I'm a dreamer, I stay determined, and I know the effects of the entire universe getting this point I'm making will be *ginormous*. Truly ginormous. So let's read on.

This is not a religious book, nor is it a self-help book. It is not meant just for Christians or for people of other faiths only. I write it in the hopes of reaching *each and every human being on the face of this earth* so we can all fully experience God's goodness and what He hopes for us to experience on this earth as our physical bodies pass through.

I am writing it for Christians, Muslims, Jews, Hindus, Buddhists, atheists, and agnostics. Pardon me if I left your religion out. But it does not really matter, for all the religions I listed are mere "labels." I am a Christian; that is my label. However, that is just a title/label, like many other titles/labels bestowed upon us at various stages of our lives.

I'm not a fan of labels. Just imagine if we didn't have to be called Christian, Muslim, atheist, and so on! Dropping labels could be the start of something big in our lives: it could completely change our outlook on other people and help us accept and understand others a lot better too.

Imagine, just for a moment, if we are all called "human beings on a spiritual path, who are seeking life's purpose, who want to know the real reason we've been placed on this earth, and who are seeking answers or clues to the mystery of life."

So while I personally do believe Jesus Christ is my Lord and Savior, my life mission is that I am just a person who will continue to seek life's meaning and continuously pursue peace. For aren't all of us searching? All of us, at every point in our lives, are seeking, questioning, and wondering about life's actual meaning.

I've met people of almost every faith label—even those who profess to no faith at all—who say things like, "I have questions"; "I'm just not sure"; "What is life really about?"; "Is there really a God?"; "Why do good people die at a young age?"; and "Why do kids get cancer?" So we are all seeking answers. As long as we are alive and have breath, we are seeking, whether we admit it or not.

Something that most of us are seeking and saying is, "I just want to be happy. How do I manage that?" Well, I believe when we say this, what we really want…is to have peace in our lives.

Peace is a continuing state of happiness, although many don't fully understand that just yet. And because they don't understand the real meaning of peace, the process of pursuing it feels completely wrong, so therefore we never experience it.

Have you ever pondered why people hate others, want to harm others, and sometimes even want to eliminate them from the face of the earth? Ultimately they think this will bring them peace if those people no longer exist. (Definitely a warped way of pursuing peace.) We all know this does not work, but strangely, their purpose was to ultimately find peace.

Why do deranged spouses want to eliminate their partners when they think they've found better choices? Their warped minds are telling them that they will find harmony and peace with the newfound love interests.

Why do robbers invade homes or banks to steal money, jewelry, and other valuables? Their warped minds are telling them they will find peace when they get possession of these items, for they will be rich and get all their needs and wants met.

Why do people envy others or hate others so deeply, often for no just cause? They hold such deep negative feelings, and this negative energy eventually hurts others. Of course, we all know these people are not pursuing peace and will not find or be able to keep it. Notice I did not write "never pursue" or "never find" peace. Fortunately, all of us have many chances—second, third, fourth, and so on.

Second Chances

You can change your life. You have the power to do it.

And so does everybody else: we can outlive our mistakes, get back in the process, and still live out our life-given purposes!

As for those groups of people who pulled themselves a hundred times away from pursuing peace due to an extreme negative act? The answer here too is yes—they can pursue peace, although they'll need to start the process all over again, and it will take them longer than other people. But they will get there eventually if that is what they desire.

There are endless examples of people who have grabbed their second chances, changed their paths, and have found peace—and inspired others to do the same.

The age we pursue peace at can make a difference in terms of our influence (you'll read a lot more about influence later in this book, as it is vital and important). For example, some of us pursue so much peace from such an early age that we are able to do incredible good during our life spans and have a widespread impact.

A perfect example of this type of person is Mattie Stepanek, who despite dealing with a rare and serious form of muscular dystrophy, inspired many people before he passed away. He lived for thirteen short years, but he wrote great poems and books that have touched countless lives.

Some of us "get it" much later in life and so pursue and touch lives, living out our purposes, for only ten or twenty years; still, how wonderful that can be! And some of us spend thirty-five or fifty or ninety years alive…and never, ever pursue peace.

But…some babies who don't make it beyond a few weeks of life may have an even greater impact on helping others fulfill their given purposes than an eighty-year-old who lived an entire life hating others and committing crimes and evil deeds. **This can happen because each and every one of us, no matter our ages, are**

powerful spiritual beings.

But how we choose to manifest our power boils down to choices.

Powerful Spiritual Beings, Powerful Choices

The choice of peace is ours, and ours alone. God wants peace for all His creation, and He has given us the power to make good choices and to keep renewing our hearts. If we start to lose track of this power within us, move away from pursuing heart issues, and start to falter, He still does not give up on any of us. That is why we have so many chances to make things right with our heart issues: God believes in all His creation, and He cares deeply for us all and is always seeking our attention so we can be transformed, renewed, and able to make better choices.

What about if each and every one of us were to choose the path of peace? I often sit down and ponder how much better this world would be if we all single handedly started to live by the fruit of the spirit. As you know, the fruit of the spirit are heart and soul issues. Living by the fruit of the spirit is for all mankind, and it is for us to be wholesome people. That's why God cares so much and loves us all so deeply. His only desire is for us to live by the fruit of the spirit, and if we do, we pursue peace. For peace cannot be found in the midst of all the noise, violence, hatred, human divisions, restlessness, lies, and chaos in this world. Thus the fruit of the spirit are in complete opposition to all the chaos.

And while I am but a speck in the human race—just a person somewhere in this universe, though a person continually seeking and determined to fulfill my life-given purpose here on this earth—I want this for you too.

Chapter 2

My Transformation

The mustard-yellow ladybug with multiple black spots made a difference in my life. It brought me hope, peace, promise, and possibility!

I was born in Lagos, Nigeria, on April 27, 1970, to two of the greatest people on the earth, my mum, Sherifat, and my dad, Ganiyu. My dad is now in the spiritual realm, so he is no longer physically here, but his spirit still lives on.

My parents were (and are) the kindest, loving, most nurturing, hardworking, ambitious, and successful people I've ever known. When I was a child, they taught me resilience, hard work, persistence, good manners, respect for my elders and authority (in fact, respect for everyone), the value of education and entrepreneurship, and how to make good choices in life. They were awesome parents, and I am so proud I was brought into this life by them and nurtured by them.

They raised me in an area of Lagos called Surulere. *Surulere* is a Yoruba word. (Yoruba is the Nigerian tribe to which I belong.) The meaning of *Surulere* is *Peace/Patience has benefits.* I am not making that up…nor is it a mere coincidence! Many incidents or happenings in our lives are not coincidences—they occur for a reason. As an example, I grew up in an area of Lagos called *Peace/Patience has benefits*, and forty-five years after my birth here I am writing a book about pursuing peace! Surprisingly, I only realized the connection between the book's title and the meaning of where I lived in my childhood as I started to write down my life story. (Let's see what else falls into place as I write and you read on.)

My family was not rich. But we lived in a good area of town, and we were comfortable. We had our extended family around us a lot. My grandmother on my mum's side, one of the sweetest souls I've known, was a fixture and influence in my life. She passed at the very ripe age of 102 twelve years ago, bless her precious soul. We had the best neighbors too. We lived in a neighborhood that was close knit, where we all looked out for each other.

As kids, my siblings and I were brought up rich in heart issues. We had awesome parents who led us on the right path and taught us life's core values. Our folks were present in our daily lives. So I had an awesome childhood, and it laid the foundation for my journey ahead.

My parents were both Muslims, and I am proud to write I was raised as a Muslim during all my formative years by both my parents, who practiced all things Islam. Now, while my parents brought all their children up Muslim—there are six of us, and I am the youngest— half of us eventually embraced the Christian faith, while the other half stayed Muslim. Our parents were comfortable with our eventual decisions of faith. They just wanted us to be happy.

My sister Jumoke, who was closest in age to me, became a Christian from middle school on. She discovered Christianity from her friends and from selecting "Bible knowledge" as one of her elective subjects in middle school and high school. She was a peaceful, calm, quiet, and introspective soul, much like my dad in temperament. She and I shared a bedroom for many years growing up, and I studied the Koran, while she studied the Bible. I watched her closely as I practiced Islam and she practiced Christianity. She is the individual who sparked a seed in me…the Christian curiosity seed.

During my childhood, I read the Koran front to back. I went to Arabic school (separate from my formal education) during my elementary, middle school, and high school years. I attended Arabic school on some evenings and weekends, and I could read and write some Arabic. I performed the holy ablution and prayed five times a day as much as I could. That was my life back then, and I was a happy soul. My connection with Islam brought me joy and peace. I was seeking, so I prayed to the creator of the universe and read the Koran. And my life worked!

My parents encouraged me to work hard, stay focused, and to always be the best I could be. They expected only excellent grades from me, as they believed in me greatly. As I also knew I had the power and ability to keep achieving high grades, I put in all the necessary work to stay at the top of my class. In particular, I enjoyed chemistry and biology. I was on a good path.

At the age of sixteen, I passed the qualifying exam for college entry with flying colors. (Yes, at sixteen!) I excelled in medical school with the influence of my parents and their words about staying focused, "reading my books," and getting a good education inspiring me all the way. I graduated a full-fledged medical doctor at the age of twenty-two.

Once I graduated, I was ready to dive in and practice. You see, I was ready to fulfill my purpose. What was that? Well, at age twenty-two, I believed it was to be a physician. I thought doing so would make me both rich and happy. And back then, that was my definition of being a successful doctor: being able to be rich and successful…and, mixed in there somewhere, healing my patients and making them feel better. Little did I know that my beliefs would totally change with time. I quickly realized that being a physician would only help me achieve life's necessities: food, shelter, and other provisions for myself and my family.

Starting My Own Family

I met my husband-to-be in medical school at the age of seventeen. We went on to date for eight years and then were married, with two beautiful, precious daughters resulting from our union. As it turned out, my husband and I would be together for a period of twenty-three years total (fifteen years of that in marriage), and I have absolutely no regrets from that union. I learned lots of wonderful lessons during those years, and they helped shape me into who I am today. (Remember, I am an optimist.)

After I met my husband, and as we became serious about our future together, we discussed raising our kids in the same faith. He told me he was Christian. *What a coincidence!* I thought. *My sister is also a Christian.* The seed was already there for me, and once I satisfied my curiosity about learning the fundamental teachings of the faith, I embarked on a different seeking path.

I asked Jesus Christ to be my Lord and Savior just a few months before the wedding. My acceptance of Jesus Christ happened at the Kensington Temple in London, England, where we were both living and practicing at the time. But please know I merely changed my "label" from Muslim to Christian; my true spiritual essence did not change. I was focused on a spiritual path…I was seeking, I was moving forward, and life was good.

Five years later, in search of greener pastures, my husband and I and moved to the States. I then went on to complete my residency at New York's Bronx–Lebanon Hospital in the South Bronx.

In the States

It was a very interesting three years of residency. From the moment I stepped in the South Bronx, I wanted to head right back to England. I was shocked by the different reality I encountered! You see, my husband and I had so much fear instilled in us about the safety of this area, and the hospital parking lot was about a half mile from the hospital. The administrative staff and other residents we knew who had enrolled before us had advised us not to walk to the hospital, even during the daytime, for fear of getting mugged! So my husband and I, as well as most of the other residents and some hospital staff, had to wait for shuttle buses to take us to and from the parking lot. At times, I even considered returning home to Nigeria.

However, those three years I spent in the Bronx ended up being some of my best years. They were busy, dynamic, and productive. I made many friends and met a diverse group of staff, physicians, and patients. I was involved with medical cases I'd only read about in textbooks, and I can proudly write that I served as chief resident in my third year (being a chief resident is usually granted in the fourth year).

But the demands on my family were grueling. My older daughter, Reni, was a toddler while we were in New York. Raising a small child while my husband and I were both adjusting to the long, tedious hours during residency was extremely tough. Good childcare was expensive, and while we tried a few live-in nannies, we didn't find one we could really trust to leave our daughter with for all those long on-call hours from Monday through Sunday. Finally, we made the difficult decision to send Reni to live with my parents in Nigeria for a year while we both finished up our second year of residency.

A few days after Reni's first birthday, my parents flew to New York to pick her up. It was bittersweet. I hated to see her go, but I was relieved knowing she would be in the nurturing hands of my parents and that my husband and I would have time to focus on our career paths.

I did not regret that decision at all. I knew I did not have a suitable alternative. I may have had to put my residency on hold until we found good childcare, and I knew this would just prolong my career path, and this was not an option for me.

Reni returned to us just before her second birthday. *Mission accomplished!* My husband and I were close to starting our third year, which was a lot less hectic time-wise. And we were able to place her in a good daycare near our home in Yonkers. So life was good and seemingly normal.

Then the 9/11 terrorist attacks happened at the tail end of my residency. I still know exactly where I was in the hospital and what I was doing that day. That incident created a big bump in our parallel lines and completely rocked our worlds. That horrific day started a new reality, and so many of us were permanently affected by the events of 9/11.

The Place to Be

Our next stop turned out to be Atlanta. My husband and I were drawn to the place from the first time we had visited the city years ago. The weather was lovely, the city was clean, and the cost of living was much lower than in New York. The apartments and homes were more spacious and affordable too. Atlanta hosted a large

Nigerian community, and several friends of ours had moved here already. It seemed like "the place to be."

In Atlanta, my dream of getting rich as a doctor grew and multiplied. My residency was done, and it was time to make the "big bucks" and be happy ever after. I felt my husband and I were on the right path. *Atlanta, here we come.*

At first I worked with an outpatient pediatric practice. Unfortunately, I was not completely happy in my first job. The position required me to cover the newborn nursery inpatient care at three different hospitals. The job turned out to not be quite what I wanted. I was restless. I had the "entrepreneurial bug" lying dormant in me somewhere, and it started to bite me. An...inner energy pushed me to explore the idea of opening my own practice. My determined, dominant personality kicked in, and oh how I *longed* to have my own practice!

Going After a Dream

I started to work toward my big dream. I purchased a book called *How to Open a Medical Practice* and read it cover to cover several times. I made notes as I read and visualized how this dream of owning a practice would unfold. I dug deep and did a lot of research.

Fast-forward—after months and months of planning, I opened my own practice in October of 2004...and it's still open today! It has grown exponentially from zero patients on day one to a busy and thriving million-dollar practice with an average of a dozen employees (including other physicians). It is exactly what I dreamed about and hoped it would be...and even more!

Finding a Ginormous Purpose

Milestone Pediatrics serves people of varied ethnicity and cultures, mostly from the lower socioeconomic class. I always say it is the "United Nations" in my practice: name one race or ethnicity, and a member of that race or ethnicity has probably walked through the doors! We serve great people and provide employment for others as well.

We serve a big refugee population—kids who are new to this country—and also those children who live in group homes and foster homes. We have a large number of volunteers who give up their time to help these kids get situated and adapt to a new and better life. They shower these children (and their families) with love and hope. My desire had been to become a rich doctor; my focus and perspective had completely changed from that! Seeing people who were so different physically in many ways interact on a spiritual/soul level changed me for the good.

I realized we are all the same people, no matter what we look like or where we're from. We are all in search of love, encouragement, peace, and validation from other human beings. This revelation changed me permanently in a positive, humbling, and hopeful way.

It's true my career has helped me make a living and earn my daily bread. But the most important part of it is all the lives I have encountered while making a living—it's been awesome. Ginormous. As it turned out, my career had a much bigger purpose: helping me interact with fellow humans and touching lives in my own special way, and constantly being touched too.

I came to truly love my profession because of all the wondrous and diverse lives placed in my path. For example, I've met the cutest babies ever. I've enjoyed meeting a seventy-year-old retired Caucasian woman who brought in four children originally from East Africa for their first doctor's visit. This woman was fulfilling her own fruit of the spirit—spreading kindness, hope, love, and peace in her own special way. It was a win-win for all.

One of the most rewarding aspects of my life also has been my choice to teach, supervise, and mentor medical students through my practice. For the past twelve years I have met a fresh new set of students and aspiring young physicians every six weeks. I have done my best to inspire and elevate them, and they have done the same in return. I have become a part of their life stories, just as they are now a part of mine. I influence them via my gifts and talents as they share with me their hopes and dreams and explore their chosen career paths.

Bumps and Curves

One year before my practice opened, I gave birth to my younger daughter, Moni. So let me paint a picture for you: I was pregnant when my practice was in the early planning stages, and I had an infant and a six-year-old while running around trying to get everything in place to open the doors of this new business I was so excited about. But I also had two beautiful children who required my full attention and affection. Suffice to say, there was a lot going on in my life. To make matters worse, my marriage was weakening. It had become quite rocky and headed south despite all my efforts! And horribly, my sister Jumoke was diagnosed with cancer and came to stay with my husband and me in Atlanta while receiving her treatments at Emory hospital.

During this stressful time, I was praying to God. But it was often distracted praying. I also was reading the Bible, but even then I remained distracted; there were just too many noises and situations going on in my head!

While I am choosing not to go into too much detail about all the humps, bumps, and curveballs that life threw me during the building and growth of my practice and for at least five years after it opened, The following diagram illustrates what my lines in my life were like.

If you look at it, you can see where my two lines (physical and spiritual) start having sharp bends and twists. I was doing all I could to keep steady and stay upright at the time, but it wasn't working! I didn't understand back then about the need to start the process of pursuing peace; all I wanted was to "be happy" again! Happy again like during my childhood days in Nigeria.

I also did not fully understand the concept of staying alive with the only two lifelines I had—my physical body and my spirit. Still, somehow I knew I had to keep taking care of my body while also nourishing my spirit as much as I could.

I had no clue that my spiritual and physical lines had to be steady and in forward motion. Despite this lack of knowledge, I did not quit or buckle during the bumps. Why? Because I still had those two lines and I was in the middle of them. My physical line was still there, and my spiritual line was also still there. Neither was at an optimal level, but they were still present.

To get through my difficult experience, I journaled. A lot. I wrote random stories and also just plainly expressed every emotion I was feeling.

Journaling was the outlet that helped me cast out a lot of the sadness and despair. Writing it all down was therapeutic through the time around my divorce (yes, the marriage fell completely apart), busy early years of my practice, and my sister's illness. As I detailed my ongoing issues and problems and current situation, I was able to grasp the overall picture a lot better—and I *knew* I had to start looking for a way out of the mess.

I was facing the fact that *it might be time to let go.* As I weighed this decision, I went to church and did all I could to fill my emptiness. I went to the gym a few days of the week or jumped on the elliptical trainer at home. I continued to eat reasonably well. I did my best to look pretty and well dressed on the outside, but inside, things weren't so pretty, because I was really struggling with so many varied thoughts. The realization that my marriage really was ending, and the fact that I had to start to navigate a new way of life for myself and my daughters was not easy.

(A brief aside: About this time, some of my friends said to me, "Oh, we had no clue you were struggling in your marriage, because you always looked cute!" Well, no matter what you are going through, it pays to look cute, even if it's just for a few hours in the day. If you look cute even when your insides are in chaos, it gives you a glimmer of hope. You have that one thing to hold on to. *So please, do not let yourself go, even in times of stress, anxiety, and unhappiness.* Imagine if you let yourself go and start binge eating and gain a lot weight. Or if you go to the other extreme and stop eating and become too skinny and frail. You then create a new set of problems for yourself, which further impacts your emotional state and your self-esteem and slows down your overall recovery. You now have just one more problem to deal with, which you do not need when life is already throwing you some pretty hard stuff! Having outer beauty and composure will help keep you moving. *So put that makeup on, tie your hair up in a ponytail or style it in the cutest hairstyle for you, don your favorite outfit, spray on your favorite fragrance, put on a pair of heels, and hold your head up high!* Men, dress up in the clothes that make you feel most confident, and be proud yet humble. All this is part of the healing process. Despite what your confused insides might be telling you, believe and act as if you are still beautiful, handsome, and awesome. Trust me—this will help you recover and get you closer to a place where everything will turn out just fine!)

As several of the fruit of *my* spirit were off at that time, I struggled to find balance. I lost control of myself and my emotions. I was impatient. I got easily angered. I isolated myself (outside of work, that is), and I was not joyful. I was not as thankful to God and the universe for all I had at the time. Yes, I had a lot, but I just could not "feel" it. I could not "see" it either. I was distracted and deeply unhappy. This was not my Creator's plan for my life, and something had to give.

Sure enough, it did. My marriage gave. Completely.

What I quit in life...was my marriage. This was not easy; I can assure you of that. I did all I could to prevent this from happening, but it just had to give. I remember ever so clearly the day I made the decision to end my marriage. I was in so much emotional pain that I got up in the middle of the morning (around 2:00 a.m.), drove to the Kroger's shopping plaza across the street from our home, and called my parents and sister in Lagos to tell them I was done. I let them know I was filing for a divorce.

I was calm. I was not the distraught, confused, and hysterical Iyabo whom they had spoken with on and off for the past several months and who was trying to push through. I had finally come to a place of peace with this decision, as I fully realized the state I was in and that I would only go downhill from here on out if I stayed.

I recognized I had too much to live for: my precious daughters, parents, siblings, practice, staff, patients, and, most importantly, *myself.* **I needed to be fully present for myself again.** I could not give all that up for one human being with whom I just could no longer make life work. I could no longer give him love, and I felt I was not receiving love from him either. I summoned up the courage, and I started the process to depart from what had become a mess.

My marriage gave, and while it took time, I eventually pulled myself together again. I consciously chose to start living by the fruit of the spirit again and to nourish my spiritual and physical lives again. I started to use my God-given gifts to elevate and inspire myself and the others around me again. I got through the incredibly tough time after the demise of a marriage and reached a better place through following those incredibly important, incredibly wonderful three steps outlined earlier.

And as I let go of the past and started to find peace and lasting happiness, love found me. This very nice man was a godsend at the time; he brought a different, refreshing, and hopeful feel to my life. He and I did a lot of traveling together, and we shared richly in each other's lives. There were still curves and bumps in my life…but at least I was back in forward motion!

A Loss

Then August of 2015 arrived. As you have already read, my father and my mother had come to Atlanta for a visit. My children really enjoyed the six weeks they spent with their grandparents. It was a good and relaxing visit for my parents too. Aside from my dad needing the help of a cane to walk because of osteoarthritis, and having lost the vision in one of his eyes from chronic glaucoma, my mum and dad were both still in reasonably good shape. My mum would still get up and dance to the Justin Bieber tunes with my teenage daughters. (She could really get her dance moves on!)

However, two weeks before my folks left for Lagos, I had a vivid dream that my dad had passed. In the dream, someone gave me the news, and I cried for a few seconds. All of a sudden though, I saw a very clear image of my father wearing a bluish-gray safari suit. He was young, with no wrinkles on his face, and he was standing upright, no cane in hand! Actually, he looked just like he did when he was in his forties and fifties. Beside him stood my older sister Jumoke, who had passed away in 2007. She was wearing a long-sleeved minty-green floral dress. I recognized that dress immediately—it had been one of my sister's favorites! My dad and sister were looking at me with huge smiles on their faces. When I noticed their expressions in the dream, my crying and sorrow immediately changed to joy and relief.

When I woke up the next morning, I called my sister Shaki in Lagos to tell her about the dream. I was troubled by it. She reassured me and said I was probably worried about our parents' health because I had been making sure to take them to their doctor's visits while they were here in the States. So after our phone conversation, I completely forgot about the dream, and it did not come to mind again.

For the remaining two weeks of my parents' visit, we had a great time. Then Moni and I accompanied my parents to the airport. We arrived a bit early, so my dad ended up having time for a long chat with his granddaughter, during which he reminded her about the importance of reading her books, studying hard, and working hard. He also reminded her to "take care of her mother." (The part about taking care of me was nice to hear! I was like, *Speak it, Dad!*)

In order for my folks to make their way through security, they both needed wheelchairs and assistance, as they could not endure the long walks through the airport. As they were being pushed through, a thought sped through my mind: *What if this is it? What if I don't see them again? They are in their eighties. They are old. Could this be it?* I quickly tucked that thought away in my mind, and my daughter and I left the airport and headed home.

Now, my dad had called me every Sunday for the past six years since my divorce to check up on me and my daughters. I noticed he did not call me on Sunday, October 11, but I didn't place a call to him that day either.

Three days later, at five in the morning, I received the kind of call no one ever wants to receive. My niece Temi was on the phone and calling me at an extremely early time for Lagos, Nigeria! None of my nieces had ever called me at such an early hour, and my heart stopped beating for a few seconds. She greeted me with, "Auntie, hold on for my mum."

My sister Shaki spoke into the phone. "Iyabo, Daddy is gone. He passed away this morning."

The phone disappeared from my hand. (I had, in fact, thrown it on the floor several feet away from me!) I started to weep and scream, and I ran to get my daughters. They both started sobbing and saying, "Grandpa, grandpa!"

My hero was gone—the calmest soul I've ever known, one of the two people who brought me into this world, and the best father any child could ever wish for.

I felt vulnerable and confused. Images and memories of him flashed through my closed eyes as I wept. A million thoughts raced about my mind every second.

As I lay in a fetal position on the floor, realizing I would never be able to fill the void his departure had left, I suddenly remembered the dream. *The dream!* The dream I had two weeks before my parents returned to Lagos…God had revealed to me that my father was going to pass away while I was in a subconscious state, a spiritual state. And now it was true, and my father and sister were together again. They were permanently happy and peaceful in the spiritual realm. Yes, their physical bodies were gone from this earth, but their spirit was still living. To know this, I had only to think about how close they had seemed to me in the dream. As if they were right beside me!

I found out my dad actually had died peacefully in his sleep that morning. He had woken up to say his prayers, enjoyed a light breakfast and tea, and then went back to take his usual midmorning nap. He never woke back up. Life would never be the same for my mother, but I was relieved to hear my father had departed from this world in the calmest manner. *A calm soul had departed in a calm way.* That fact carved a smile on my face amid all the sorrow and pain.

Tuning In and Connecting

Even though I had not seen my dad every day since I moved away from Nigeria, I still felt an incredible void from his passing. I realized he and I had remained connected in a strong way spiritually even when I was living on the other side of the world from him!

Since we were able to remain connected while he was living, I did not want to accept the idea that I would now lose that connection because of his death. I remembered the dream, and I accepted we truly are spirits and that our spirits are stronger than our flesh, than our bodies. The knowledge changed me forever.

I made a decision to keep the connection with my father strong by dedicating some time every morning to pray for his soul and my mum's peace and comfort; read the Bible and meditate on its words of truth; and journal. I had been journaling before my father's death, but not consistently. Now I started to journal on a daily basis again.

I began to pray in the quiet of my closet and connected to God in the quiet of my bedroom. I really tuned in to my prayers as I asked God for peace and meaning.

Each morning from then on out, I connected with my father and with God on a deeper level. I wrote down affirmations. These are positive phrases that describe what we want and are hoping for in our lives; we repeat them to ourselves and believe that they will come to pass. I canceled out noise and focused in deeply.

I did the same at bedtime. When my kids were asleep or not home, I lit candles and prayed. I needed the peace and quiet to cancel out distractions and really tune in.

As a result of my new focus, I felt my dad's presence surrounding me all the time. It was a comforting, warm feeling; I knew he was next to me and that I need not worry anymore.

One November evening, as I was praying in the candlelit quiet of my home with my eyes shut, an intense brightness began shining through my closed eyes. There was an image of a tall bearded man dressed in all-white robes from his head to his feet. His face was not fully clear to me, but he was carrying a cross so big it extended from his chest to the ground. It was made of glass so brightly lit that it sparkled and glowed like a huge star in the sky.

To the right of this tall person was my dad! He was dressed exactly as he was in the dream I had before he passed, in a bluish-gray safari suit. To the left of the man was my sister; she too was dressed in the same attire as in my September dream.

35

All three of these people were smiling as they looked at me.

I felt a peace and joy I had never felt before. I was reassured that both my father and my sister were in a good place. Even though my eyes still were closed, I could sense and see brightness all around me.

I will let you make your own conclusions as to who the tall man dressed in white was. As for me, I was convinced he was a person of peace, a person from a higher realm. I believe he was the Holy Spirit.

Life went on. I continued connecting with my spiritual side. The consistent quiet prayer and journaling sessions brought me a feeling of peace and the warmth of my dad's presence.

The Messenger

It was a Monday night in December 2015, after I had finished praying. As I lay in bed ready to fall asleep, I heard a plopping sound on my bedroom blinds. I got up to take a closer look. It was a ladybug! I shook the blind, and the insect fell on the carpet. My instinct was to kill it.

As I picked up a book to smash it, I noticed its beauty: it was a mustard-yellow ladybug sporting multiple black spots. I immediately stopped, laid the book down, and watched as it crawled on my carpet. After admiring its beauty for a bit, I went to back to bed. As I dozed off, I thought, *The sound it had made on the blind was pretty loud for such a small insect. Hmmm…it must really have been trying to get my attention!*

The next night when I lay down to sleep, the light in my closet was partially illuminating my room. I was all tucked in, but I spied something from the corner of my eye that was crawling on the wall right beside my headboard. It was the yellow ladybug again. *The same one…yellow with black spots!* I smiled and went to sleep.

When I rose on Wednesday, I did so thinking about the insect's consistent appearance. *It could not be here in my home again and again due to pure coincidence!* My daughters and I lived on the sixth floor in an apartment building in the city. *How was this ladybug getting up here?* We never leave any of our windows or doors open, and it was winter! Plus, our windows have double insulators. In the three years we have lived in this apartment, we have never, ever seen a ladybug. Especially one in my bedroom always around the same time, and two days in a row! And it wasn't even a red one, but a yellow one. Honestly, I did not even know yellow ladybugs existed; I'd only seen pictures of red ones in books, and only spied red ones when at the park and or in the garden. *And why was the insect only showing up around my bedtime?*

Wednesday night approached, and I was in my room with my laptop on my lap. I was finishing up my last bit of work for the night. My eyes were tired, and I was ready to close my laptop, when my newfound friend crawled from my sheets and slowly up onto my laptop!

Okay, this simply could not be mere coincidence. Three nights in a row? It had to mean something.

I immediately started researching ladybugs on the Internet… Did you know ladybugs are a messenger of promise and a sign of luck? They appear to reconnect us with the joy of living. One of the messages that the ladybug brings to us is that we need to release our fears and return to love. Wow!

I read on, only to encounter stories of people seeing ladybugs after their loved ones had passed, or during times of deep prayer and reflection. I also discovered these other meanings that ladybugs have:

- They are a sign of abundant blessings.

- The number of dots on the ladybug signifies the number of blessings a person will get. (Wow, I really liked that one. Come on, blessings. I'm ready to receive you with open hands!)

- The spiritual meaning of the ladybug is spiritual devotion. (Spiritual devotion? Another wow. This is getting better, Iyabo, I told myself. You have a spiritual side, and it is manifesting itself to you through your visions, dreams, and now through your new friend, the ladybug!)

During this time period, I encountered my new friend for a fourth time. When Saturday arrived, my daughter Moni and I were sitting at the park on a bench outside our apartment building. All of a sudden my daughter said, "Look, Mum. It's your friend the ladybug! It's next to you. Look!"

Well, that ladybug crawled right beside my leg on the bench before it dropped to the ground and flew away. It was still the same one: yellow with multiple spots.

Ladybug, I'm glad you are in my life, especially now that I know what you mean. I'll be happy if you keep paying me frequent visits!

I have not seen my friend since that time. But I believe it came to me back then to give me hope, love, joy, and an assurance of peace for my dad. It helped remove the fear of the physical absence of my dad and further delivered the message of the strength of my spiritual side. It came to comfort me and let me know I would be just fine. My fears were being replaced...with hope and joy!

The ladybug had served me with a spiritual message. It had come to assure me that what I could not see with my naked eye—love, hope, joy, and a future even better than that—was actually present in my life. Now I love ladybugs. The mustard-yellow ladybug with multiple black spots truly made a difference to my life. It brought me hope, peace, promise, and possibility.

(And now you know why there are ladybugs on the chapter opener pages throughout this book! To honor ladybug moments in our lives, moments of strength, hope, love, and breakthrough. These are the kind of moments I hope everyone will experience!)

A New Way of Living

I now was on a mission...a mission to *keep exploring my spiritual side*. The still, quiet, prayer-filled candlelit journaling sessions were not only bringing me peace, joy, comfort, and clarity. They also were bridging the gap between my spiritual and physical lives!

Too, I had found out that the consistent practice of these sessions was helping me live a better life. *I truly was living by the fruit of the spirit.* Yes, I was already doing so before my father passed, *but not consistently and not without distractions.* Before my dad had died, my mind would run through a million differing thoughts as I prayed and journaled. I was so easily distracted: by chores, my kids, the medical practice, deadlines, and life in general. I was not fully *in tune.*

However, after my dad passed, I was more conscious of canceling out noise and fully immersing myself in trying to connect with him and God. I so wanted to hold on to the strong connection I had had with my father when he was still alive. At the same time, I was so much more conscious of living by the fruit of the spirit in my daily life, and I liked what I was experiencing. It felt peaceful and promising. I was on my process of pursuing peace.

I realized I must continue to nourish my spiritual side daily and always. When I did, my life felt so good, so balanced. I am a spiritual being; indeed we all are! *My goodness, this was something. I must share this with the world...*

The Creation

I started to get this strong, intense longing and urge to put all of my recent experiences into words. I needed to write all my experiences down. I had neither a plan nor any experience with structured writing. The only type of writing I had been doing was journaling!

Thoughts and ideas of all sorts started filling my brain, everywhere and anywhere. I had a burning desire to write! I made notes on my phone and on pieces of scrap paper. I even stepped out of the shower when content rushed into my head to get it transcribed and preserved!

At 5:00 a.m. I would wake up with loads of ideas and content welling up in my thoughts. Immediately I would jot it all down. Before I fell asleep, the same thing would happen: an incredible flood of content would make its way into my thoughts. As I wrote, I noticed *I could not stop.* I believed I was meant to write this book; the creation process was too automatic to not be real!

I looked forward to quiet time alone, just so I could get lost in penning my thoughts. The chapters came easily, and I typed away. The material started to shape into a book, word by word, sentence by sentence. Within two months, I had effortlessly written fifty-six thousand words!

The book I started to write on December 15, 2015, was done before February 20, 2016. And what I had created was a book detailing how, if you totally tune in with your spirit by having quiet, still times, prayer times, and affirmation times, you will connect with the highest spirit—God—and gain clarity in your life. In turn, this would help you live your life according to the fruit of the spirit. You would start to pursue peace, and this process would touch others, so you would start to make a difference in this world.

Connecting with your spirit and having quiet time can be done in many ways. The main denominator turned out to be…canceling out noise, chaos, chores, deadlines, kids, financial issues, worries, and the phone, TV, and other devices while you are in your quiet, still, reflective times. You cannot tune in with your spirit while your mind is racing at a hundred miles an hour! I suggest starting with fifteen minutes a day and increasing the time incrementally until it reaches one hour daily.

Chapter 3

Be the Change Our Children Need

Having kids is not a hobby, novelty, pastime, or form of therapy. It is serious business!

Our children are bundles of innocent joy, arriving into this world with gifts given to them by our Creator.

In my quiet times, I always wonder how babies, such bundles of joy, purity, and goodness, can transform into such different human beings. *How and why do beautiful babies grow up and turn into murderers, convicts, robbers, and/or drug addicts?* This transformation is sad and one I have seen far too many times in my career as a pediatrician.

This kind of transformation often can happen at the hands of adults not equipped to raise babies or young children appropriately. So little ones who started out as bundles of innocent joy began interacting with, experiencing, and internalizing the negative influences of the world through the eyes, attitudes, and hands of these adults.

And sometimes the negative influences on our children come from other kids! It is sad if we consider the high number of peer influences out there that are detrimental. Those children holding these attitudes and behaviors are this way because back when they were little, they had interacted with incompetent parents, caregivers, or guardians who were not positive forces in their lives. And unfortunately, they will probably grow up to misguide and negatively impact their own children one day, even though they might try their best to lead their kids in the right direction. It is a vicious cycle that we see happening time and again.

To combat this, we must stay in the middle of our lines alone. We must nourish our spiritual and physical lines to keep them straight and in forward motion in order to help our kids nourish *their* own lines as they grow up into adults and leave us to live their own lives one day. We cannot have our kids in the middle of our own lines; they have their own!

Your six-month-old baby cannot be in the middle of your lines with you. Your five-year-old who needs you cannot be in there with you. Neither can your fifteen-year-old teenager! You cannot squeeze your kids in. Nope! They are all in the middle of their own lines. They are all-powerful spiritual beings who just happen to have a physical body for now, and as you are aware, each spiritual being stays in the middle of his or her own lifelines.

The faster we come to terms with this phenomenal truth that we alone are flanked on either side by our lifelines, the faster we will be able to do all that it takes to pursue peace and be permanently happy. And in terms of our children and how they can become permanently happy: Our children must see us, observe us, and feel us actively working on living by the fruit and nourishing our lifelines. Only then will they grow up to be balanced individuals who have learned how to nourish their own lifelines and pursue peace.

Children therefore must have good parental influences in order to make it in life. If their parents are not working on love, joy, self-control, gratitude, forgiveness, and moving toward the peace process, they will bring up children who cannot find this fruit or pursue this fruit for themselves.

Looking Out for All Children

Some of us have children whom we give birth to and who are our biological children. Some of us adopt children who are not genetically ours but whom we bring into our lives and who become family. And many of us have biological, fostered, and adopted children in our families!

Ideally, we have all these kinds of kids in our lives. Now, I am not saying everyone should adopt or foster children. However, we must take care and be sure we are influencing *not only those children who belong to our own families, but also the other children out there, as they need positive influences in their lives.*

So many children in our world today need mentoring, guiding, and inspiring. The number of children around the world whose God-given gifts are being annulled is unbelievable, and we adults must take action. Children really need adults who are living out the pursuit of peace in order to understand that they can embark on the process too. There are too many children who desperately need mentors, and we are not satisfying their need fast enough.

Be the change. Use your gifts, resources, and time in any combination to positively impact our children.

It's quite all right to start small. For example, you can start in your immediate community whenever you can, wherever you are, and with whatever resources you have. How?

We can influence others and spread our wisdom and knowledge in two ways. The first is by communicating with people by talking to them or through the written word: books, magazines, editorials, e-books, blogging, and other forms of literature.

The second is by letting others observe us—and when it comes to children, *this second way is a lot more effective.* Let our kids see us acting as responsible adults who are living by the fruit of the spirit and living out our life-given purposes…and they will be inspired to do the same!

Pointing a Finger

For those of us who have children who aren't behaving as we hope, I am going to write something you may not want to read: we place a bit too much responsibility on the school system, the community, and the government to help us in raising our kids. For example, many of us verbally instruct our kids to behave a certain way but then go on to behave a totally different way ourselves, which we feel is acceptable because we are the adults. Then we go on to point the finger at the school or another party for not being able to influence our children in the desired manner, even though we ourselves are not being good or strong role models.

This mindset has to change. We can't continue to point the finger at some other person, group, and/or institution, expecting them to be the responsible party for raising our own kids! Let me give you an example that I encounter all too frequently. In my years of pediatric practice, where I am interacting with patients, parents, and caregivers, there is a particular kind of hypocrisy played out time and again. This occurs when obese parents bring in their kids to my office and strongly scold their overweight or obese kids in front of me because I am informing them of their children's conditions. "Are you listening to the doctor?" they will say. "*She* says you should stop eating all that junk food they let you eat at school!"

Why should so much blame go to the school? If you are a parent who is overweight or obese and you are blaming your 180-pound twelve-year-old for getting into that state because she eats junk food at school, you are completely missing the mark: As long as you remain overweight or obese, so will your children. You must take action for your health, and then your child will see and then follow the good example!

In all my years of practice, I have not encountered an overweight or obese pediatric patient whose parents are at a healthy, normal weight. Let me write—with respect, humility, and gentleness—it is the parents' fault if their children become obese. It is not the fault of the school, the society, or the system at large. You cannot keep gaining fifteen pounds or more every year and not expect your child to do the same! You buy the food and stock the pantry. You prepare most of the meals (probably), and if there is fast food/soda, usually you are the one paying for this. Obesity does not just "run in" your family. Nor is it the result of "heavy bones." Be honest with yourself, and stop being in denial about what is causing the obesity.

If you teach your kids about good nutrition and healthy eating at home, and you set a good example they can observe daily, they will make good food choices at school and wherever they may go without you. Your kids are watching you. They will do as you do, not as you say. So until you start doing together, there is no getting out of this. **Start making changes step by step as a family.**

Our children need to see the change in *us.* Let us take responsibility for the nurturing of our children and stop blaming everything and everybody else.

Our Mirrors

The examples of ways in which our children pick up negative traits from us are endless. So many of us parents and other adults want our kids to get a good education, stay focused, get a good job, stay the course, and be resilient so that they can become fulfilled and successful adults. However, when our kids observe us, they often spy us doing and acting in ways that are the exact opposite of these goals! As examples: How many of us make excuses for not getting up to go to work? Have we ever said our job is "not good enough," and then, when we stay at home, we are miserable and unsatisfied? Or have we jumped from one menial job to another, never putting our heart into the work and not trying enough to be good at what we are supposed to be doing?

Well, you can talk to your kids as much as you like about why they should do well in school, and why they should never give up...but if you do not live out the example of hard work, resilience, and perseverance to live out your passion and dreams, you will be surprised what your kids will do in the future when they are adults. Maybe they'll start out with a good education like you did, but then they might end up making excuses as to how there is "no suitable" job for them and decide to simply stay at home and laze about every day. Or they may not even stay the course for a good education! They may drop out of school, as they have seen your apathy when it comes to getting and keeping a good job, and they may devalue education.

Be careful, adults. Our children are our mirrors. They will reflect us as they grow up. Be their light and a mirror of hope so that our children see us striving, and they start to strive even harder themselves.

Get up and out of the chair! We need to start doing and positively influencing so that our children will be doers and positive influencers too.

The Correct Answer

How do children learn bad manners and disrespect for others? How and where do they learn to be rude and aggressive and to act out at people of authority? How do they learn to speak with foul language? How do they learn to be violent and commit crimes? How do they learn to be intolerant of people who do not look or act like them? How do they learn how to dress inappropriately? How do they learn to be negative and apathetic about life in general? From their parents and other significant adults around them!

Sure we can blame all the nasty behaviors exhibited by our children on social media, TV, school, other friends, negative music, history, the government, the system, and past influences as much as we want. But those answers are *wrong*, and this kind of misguided blaming is the main reason for the majority of our ongoing societal problems. It is the easy way out for a lot of parents and adults not involved in a child's life.

In particular, the schools, teachers, and other students are *not* the causes of a child's obesity, bad eating habits, poor behavior, inappropriate mode of dressing, disrespect of authority, violence, criminal acts, drug use, teenage pregnancy, and all the other problems plaguing our precious kids these days. The problem starts *at home.* A child's actions, behaviors, and beliefs may be *exaggerated* by school influences and the society at large, but they always start *at home.* It's certainly true teachers are an important influence in all our kids' lives, but they are not the parents. They are just an adjunct to our kids' futures.

Adults and parents are the responsible caregivers of the child, and so they are to blame. Regardless of the other influences and chaos of this world, if we teach our kids well by example, invest our time in them, and are engaged and fully present in their formative years, they will turn out to be good citizens of the world who will live by the fruit of the spirit (just like their parents). Even if they make missteps or bad decisions or choices for a while, they eventually will remember their foundation and reset their lives back in a positive direction.

We chose to bring our children into this world, so we are the ones who must be responsible to help them notice their gifts and then teach them how to keep their physical and spiritual lives flowing and how to live a life of magnificence and influence. We must be more responsible parents and cease blaming everybody else and every outside influence.

If Our Best Attempts Aren't Enough, Then What?

We could be doing our best to raise honorable kids, but our kids may unfortunately fall prey to other kids who have absent, careless, and/or clueless parents. As parents raising good kids, if our kids fall into a bad cycle with other kids, there goes all our efforts. How do we understand and address this?

If we all as adults are fully aware that we are not just raising our own kids but other people's kids indirectly because our kids inevitably mingle with other children, it will solve the majority of our world problems! It honestly does take a village to raise and nurture a kid…but a village that is wise, morally sound, and steadfast.

Let Go and Let In

Parents, please realize your children are observing and watching if you stay in a physically, verbally, and/or emotionally abusive marriage or relationship. Doing so will be something that destroys their souls and spirits. Are you fully aware of the damage that is being done to them? It is often an irreversible hurt that will continue to confuse, deter, and prevent them from living their life-given purposes in the future.

Some victims of abuse offer up the rationale of, "I am staying strong for my kids," or, "I don't believe in divorce," or, "I believe in God, and He will bring me a miracle!" for choosing to stay in what is an abusive relationship. While all such statements may well be true, it is my professional and personal opinion that if you have done all you can within your power—sought counseling and family therapy, prayed to your higher power, and given the relationship reasonable time—please **let go and let in.** Let go of the continued abuse, free yourself and your kids from this horrific torture, and begin to renew yourself step by step. If you are free of this hurtful relationship, one day you may be able to let in a partner who truly deserves you! There are indeed good and honorable people out there, and many of them are looking for people to honor with their love and trust. It often is all about timing. You deserve the best, and *the best will come to you with time and with patience.* Here though, I must make an exception when it comes to physical abuse*: the very first time you are hit, please make your exit.* (Strategically, of course, so that you minimize the risk to yourself and your family.)

That person hitting you has extremely unstable lifelines that are having major twists and bends, and it will require a very long process for that person to get their lines back in a steady forward-motion state. You cannot and should not sit around while this process is going on, as you will continue to be the punching bag and catalyst for their extreme emotional states. The abuser needs extreme intervention, and so you must make your exit. You can figure out how to best do this by contacting an abused/battered woman's hotline and/or talking to trusted mentors, family members, and friends.

Remember: make your way out carefully and as soon as possible.

How Abuse Affects Kids

You may be surprised to know how scared and fearful children get while observing a parent stay in an abusive situation. Children do not deserve to experience, watch, and become a part of all that is going on. If you are choosing to stay in the relationship, you are scaring your own children. *Please stop!*

After my divorce, several people asked why I just didn't "hang in there" for my children's sake, as it "was not good" for kids to experience divorce. I must write that their question truly puzzled me. Well, I "left and let go" because I wanted my precious innocent daughters to know that I had had enough of the emotional and verbal ups-and-downs and back-and-forth that had continued for years. They needed to be aware that I still had the power in me that was strong enough to enable me leave, choose better, and do better. I wanted to show my daughters that they deserve only the best, and they do not have to "make do" if their lives are spiraling out of control. If they have done all they can, they must *let go and let in.* My daughters had seen enough and heard enough negative words, and it was time to start the healing and renewal process for all three of us. Time to get my lifelines back to flowing steadily in *forward* motion. Time for peace/permanent happiness!

Years later, I still am so glad I made the decision I did. I also remain grateful to one of my greatest influencers and mentors: my dad. At one point, after having seen or heard about all the ups-and-downs I had experienced over the years, my father sat down quietly beside me one day and said, "Iyabo, if you have done all you can, and you want to move on with your daughters, please do it. Move out of this house; you are too unhappy." Those words sunk into the very base of my soul and empowered me! My father was not a quitter, and he never, ever had encouraged me to quit before, so I knew he said those words only because he could see I was in an unhappy and hurting state. He could tell I was hitting the point of no return in that union.

I am sad to write that my mum—who I had thought would be the one who would say this to me at the time—didn't feel the same. She was overwhelmed and saddened by the situation and quite panicked with fear that it would negatively impact my daughters if I moved out of the house and left my marriage. I know both my parents loved me and wanted only the best for me and my family, but it was the calmness behind, and gentle strength of, my father's words that empowered and inspired me.

Our Power to Change

Parents, caregivers, and other adults, our children are watching, observing, and listening to everything about us. Let us start to set good examples for them. Our children are the future, and the future is extremely important!

It is unfortunate if your life did not turn out the way you hoped for up to this point because of various situations and influences beyond your control, but please know that you can still start to make active changes and shifts to turn your life around…and you can allow your children to see you making those changes. Let your kids see you get up and turn your life around!

Do not sit around blaming the society, your boss, your spouse or ex, the government, groups of people, the past, your parents, and others for your situation. **Get up, let go, and let in.** You are responsible for you, and you have the power within you to change. Enough with laziness, worry, fear, lies, self-pity, and misplaced blame on others. *You can transform your life and live the life of your dreams and the life you truly deserve. Your children need to see you doing this.*

Do not stay in a miserable and unsatisfying situation and then try to teach your kids not to make the same mistake and to do better for themselves. *That never works!* They will do what you do, not what you say, unless they have a great influencer outside of their home who empowers and strengthens and gives them hope. (This is rare, but it does happen to the few kids who really identify the problem in their homes and go out seeking the truth with great influencers other than their parents and immediate family.)

This is why we all must be influencers of children: we never know the impact we could make in the life of that one child who is struggling with a difficult home situation, wherein we become the light of permanent change in that child's world.

Teen Time

Teenagers and other adolescents: You are still on a path of learning, discovery, and growth. You are still children who are not yet equipped mentally, emotionally, financially, and sometimes physically to take up the raising of a child. Any children born to you at this age will have a very hard time starting off in life.

Each and every child is born with precious gifts, and children need *adults* living by the fruit of the spirit and nourishing their physical and spiritual lines to help them navigate through their lives. As teenagers, you are not yet equipped to do this, as you still need ongoing positive influencing in your own lives!

Please don't choose to have a child because you are unhappy, want to prove something to someone, or desire to have someone to love and who loves you in return! *Babies are not a form of therapy.* Having babies at a very young age or having multiple babies back to back when you are obviously not emotionally or spiritually ready will not make you happy. Babies are not a solution to your woes and hopelessness.

If you are going through hard, unstable times and battling self-esteem issues, and you fall prey to lust, have unprotected sex, and have a baby, you have made your whole situation *ten times worse.* Now there is not just you to "fix" and get back on track, but you have an innocent baby who has to live through this situation you are still battling.

You can find and enjoy companionship with a girlfriend or boyfriend, start building a relationship, *and postpone having sex until the time is truly right.* Do you fully understand what you are doing by having unprotected sex without a solid plan for taking care of the baby that may result from this one act? Do not place yourself in that vulnerable situation alone with your boyfriend or girlfriend. *Grasp on to the power and self-control that lies within you and say no to sex sternly, respectfully, and with gentle confidence.*

And really, you have only two choices: you can stay abstinent (that is, say no), or have sex *with contraception* as well as *condoms.* There are no in-betweens; *you have your whole future in front of you.* You should only have babies when the time is right and when you have the solid plan, resources, relationship, and partner to take care of a child. You need wisdom, growing time, a significant other who will help support you, your own success and fulfillment, your peace pursuit, an education, and a job. *All these child-rearing necessities must come together to raise a child properly.*

So ask yourself this question before having sex if you are a teenager: "If I get pregnant [or get her pregnant] and have a baby, do I have all the resources and time needed to help this baby manifest its God-given gifts to magnificence?" **If your answer is no, you should be**

abstaining from sex.

Please be honest with yourself as you answer the question. All babies are destined for magnificence and significance, so if you are not equipped to fully support a child in achieving this, please abstain from unprotected sex.

Actually, abstain altogether. Abstinence from sex will not lead to your demise. Trust me. It will not. **You will not die if you are not having sex.** Your boyfriend or girlfriend will not leave you if you are not having sex with them. Or if they do, they were not worth your while in the first place!

Sometimes our hormones tell us we just must be having sex all the time, but please connect with your *soul.* Your soul and spirit will free you from this attachment with sex and the need for jumping from person to person for sex to fulfill a higher need that they cannot provide for you.

I have practiced abstinence from sex many a time, and I am still alive! And I am quite thankful that I did.

If you are not in a steady, loving, committed relationship, you should not be having sex. Teenagers, it takes time to find and develop such relationships. Slow down and focus on what is important. Keep your eye on the great future ahead of you, and focus and work on how to get there without distractions.

If you do make the irreversible mistake of getting pregnant and having a baby, please learn from your mistake and do not repeat the process.

This is a trap teenagers fall into time and time again. Over the years, I have seen teenage patients of mine become mothers, then go on to have another child (or more) back to back. I'm referring to fourteen-, fifteen-, and sixteen-year-olds having two or more kids (from different fathers) in a period of three to five years! As for the fathers, who are often teens themselves, they often show up for the first appointments and then completely vanish from their children's lives thereafter.

Sadly, the teenage moms have to drop out of school, and they cannot keep a job, as raising a child is quite a responsibility at such a young age. Unfortunately, teenagers quickly get overwhelmed, and they cannot combine school, work, and their new responsibility effectively. School and work fall off, and then their emotional, spiritual, and physical worlds also get weakened. A few go on to commit a crime and may even end up in jail. Their babies end up being raised by the grandparents who still have their own lives to live (as many of them are only in their thirties).

Eventually, as they get older, these children of teens end up in foster homes or group homes who do try their best for these kids, but such homes also have their own limitations and shortcomings. (There is only so much these homes can do. They try their best, and communities do need them. However, nothing compares to the love and nurturing of an emotionally and spiritually sound parent.)

Collective Power

And now we have come to one of those ladybug moments (see the previous chapter if you need a "bug refresher"): It is up to us to stop this vicious cycle. We have the power to do it, one great influencer at a time. My hope is that every person reading this book is not defensive but, instead, turns introspective, analyzing how they are living their lives and proceeding to do their parts in being a positive influence on children, raising them properly, and helping them manifest their God-given gifts to magnificence.

Being defensive, criticizing my intent, or judging me because of my observations without pondering your unique life situation doesn't help anybody. Critical and judgmental people are the ones who never make any positive changes, and subsequently they never get out of the messes they are in!

Humility always wins. Please be humble, and examine all the truth in my words carefully. We must *collectively* stop the cycle, one teenager at a time, one adult at a time, and one step at a time.

During the process, we will be making key shifts and essential changes. We will be true to ourselves, examining the role we play in all of this and no longer laying the blame on everybody else, society, and circumstances. If we do this, we eventually will transform the world, community by community!

Absence and Disorder Doesn't Make the Heart Grow Fonder

Many problems plaguing our societies today with regard to children stem from a lack of responsible home education. There are way too many physically absent parents—as well as physically present but emotionally and spiritually unavailable parents.

It breaks my heart, and concerns me greatly, when the media, and other people, speak up on TV or a radio show and focus on the problems facing our teens and adolescents yet fail to tackle or examine the state of our children in their formative years from zero through thirteen. Those are our kids' most important developmental years, so why do we continue to do this? Why aren't we first discussing the problems that occur from zero to thirteen, and then beyond? And during those crucial shaping years…who is responsible for leading a child in the right direction before common teenage problems surface?

By now you are aware that answers like "school," "our society," "the government," and "the world" all fall into the "wrong" category. The parents who decided to birth that child are the responsible parties! If every parent is mindful that as they raise their own children right, they need to also be raising other parents' kids right, we will all be headed in a positive and inspiring direction.

Now, I used the term "home education" earlier. I would like to point out that I mean something quite different by this than the term "homeschooling," wherein parents are taking the academic place of a school-based teacher and instructing their children at home. What I mean by "home education" is what happens when *present and engaged parents are engaged in wise and positive interactions on almost every subject imaginable with their children as well as the children of others.* We must invest our time and energy into nurturing our children! Otherwise, juvenile delinquency, youth violence, poverty, crime, apathy, misplaced anger, and division on all levels stem from the parenting that happens during a disordered state.

What do I mean by a "disordered state" when it comes to parenting? It refers to a *stage or state of affairs in which we are not ready, on many levels, to bring into, and care for, the children of this world.* For example, is it worthwhile to chase after career advancement, money, and all the material things of this life if, in the doing, we are neglecting or misguiding our children? Is it all right if our children end up with major problems because we are absent physically, emotionally, and/or mentally? If we are still struggling with financial and career independence in life, should we be having multiple kids back to back?

There are way too many families out there having children they cannot take care of or provide for.

If you have four kids and are earning minimum wage, chances are you will have to take on three (or more) jobs, which include night and weekend shifts, to pay the bills so that your family has the necessities of life. Well, then you end up having no time to spend with your kids, and they end up navigating life by themselves. And if you get home suffering from chronic exhaustion and immediately crash in bed, you are not spending quality time with your kids. They will fail in school, have major behavioral problems, and disrespect authority. Their lives will spiral out of control because they are not receiving love and guidance from you. If you are not around and are always chasing after your jobs and other daily life distractions, you end up with kids who have major social and psychological issues. And so the vicious cycle continues...

Our innocent kids truly and deeply need to be nurtured and taken care of by us. They need us around to love, nurture, guide, influence, and teach them how to be the best they can be and how to use the gifts they were born with to magnificence. Of course it is absolutely fine if we need to put our kids in daycare or with a sitter, nanny, relative, or friend for part of the day while we work or go to school. But when we do so, we then must be sure to spend some time every day to connect and bond with our own children...*and we must be very present when we do so.*

Planning Ahead

Having kids is not a game, novelty, or some form of therapy or self-achievement. Raising and nurturing a child is a very big decision. You must have a plan for how to provide, nourish, guide, and love your children until they are adults and "set free" with all the tools necessary to live their own lives effectively. It does not work well if done in reverse; you cannot have five kids and then start running around trying to make ends meet. You will ruin your life and those poor kids' lives as well. (It is called "family planning" for a reason!)

Plan your own life first. Get an education, use your God-given gifts, learn a skill, finish with flying colors, get a career you love, work on your spiritual and physical lifelines, and *then* start to plan on having a baby. This works; the reverse does not. Plan first, put your plan into action, and then have children (and by the way, I mean a *reasonable* number of children, or in other words, an amount of children that you can effectively provide for while still taking care of yourself). My assumption here is that you also have a supportive spouse beside you helping you with nurturing these kids.

Having children with multiple partners is not a good idea. I've seen women in my practice who have had five kids with five different men, and those men are absentee fathers. This is a sure recipe for disaster—and yet this very thing happens way too often these days. We can do better. We *must* do better. It is time.

Women, if you have one child with one man and he disappears and is not involved with the upbringing of that child, why do you keep repeating that mistake over and over again? I believe there is an emotional void somewhere deep in your soul that you must immediately come to terms with. What are you fearful of? Where is the insecurity coming from? What deep-seated hurt are you trying to numb by having multiple children?

One or a combination of the three components of finding permanent happiness is missing in your life. Please start to immediately journal, writing all your thoughts and differing emotions down. If you do, soon you will discover where the problem lies. And when you do, you must stop making this a recurring problem in your life! Take charge of the power in you, and *make better choices.* Having kids is one of the greatest responsibilities in life.

If you simply are not capable of providing time, wisdom, love, and life's needs for your kids, please abstain from sex. Instead, get busy with your spiritual and physical lines, and work on yourself first before bringing babies into the mix.

If the Unexpected Happens

If you unexpectedly end up alone in terms of taking care of your children—like me—this is all the more reason to be wise and plan strategically to give them the best you can on your own.

Recognize that our children need us around fully present and engaging with them for some hours *every single day!* So spend some time sharing your day with each other. Hold hands. Pray with your kids in the morning. Say affirmations before you all head out the door. Have dinner together when you all return home, or if that's not possible, set aside a special "dessert" time a few times a week where family members talk about what's on their minds and what's been going on in their lives. You'll be amazed at what kinds of conversations may result. Enjoy fun family activities together over the weekend, whether it's tossing a baseball, reading together, or grooving to a dance tune. Be silly and goofy together.

Love Them; Hold Your Ground

We must be our children's biggest advocates. We must believe in our children and encourage them to be the best. We must remind them of how great they can become if they stay focused and work hard in school and be respectful of others as well as any form of authority.

So do not put your child down with negative words. Even if you "lose your cool" sometimes and say what you do *not* mean, please apologize to them later and let them know that what you just said was done in "the spur of the moment" and you are sorry.

Our children are trying to process so much information from so many influences—good and bad—that they often get confused. *Parents and responsible adults must bring clarity to them and help them navigate through the good and bad.* We must speak words of hope, truth, encouragement, and love. We must praise them when they do well and correct them when they err. We must appropriately discipline with love and place them back on the right path when they make mistakes. We must always stand up for the truth with our kids. If they are on the wrong path, we must, as parents, hold our ground and lead them back into a positive direction, no matter what that takes.

Balance and plan out your life so that you have time to attend important meetings at your child's school and their sports and creative performances. Cheer them on, and express your pride in them. Get to know their friends and their friends' families. *The company they keep will shape their futures.* Be very careful and discerning of sleepovers you allow them to go to and of any children you allow into your home. Allow this kind of close contact only with like-minded families. Ask questions before they go on sleepovers: Who will be supervising the kids? Is anyone else visiting who does not live with them? Will they be swimming, and if so, will an adult be present? Do the parents keep guns at home, and if so, are they safely locked away? Otherwise you will be surprised that your ten-year-old child is with other ten-year-olds upstairs looking at porn while the supervising adult—say, a grandparent—is asleep in the basement. Or you may find out your eight-year-old was playing with a loaded gun. Or a visitor who may be a pedophile may be allowed in the home.

Advocate for your child's safety, health, and spiritual well-being. Be alert and wise, and listen to your spirit when it is telling you something is not right somewhere with regard to your kids.

Emptying Out Noise

I have had instinct after instinct with regard to the lives of my daughters—and those instincts have always turned out to be true and justified. I have even had dreams signaling me to talk to my kids about some issues…and those issues turned out to be actually going on!

The most recent one happened while I was at a workshop listening to the speaker. A vision flashed across my mind of my younger daughter falling and hurting herself during basketball practice. (To set the stage: earlier in the morning Moni had been taken to her school for basketball practice by her older sister.) Well, within a minute of this vision, a text popped up on my phone from one of the moms at the practice informing me my daughter had fallen and sprained her ankle. *Wow!* I thought. *I am glad I was here quietly listening to a speaker and fully connected in the moment, as I was open to receiving God's notice. Because of that, He gave me prior notice before this text came in!*

God loves His children. He wants to keep them safe, and He wants to do it through us.

Stay connected with your spirit so you can be connected to God, who will show you how to protect and nurture your kids. You cannot discern God if you are running helter-skelter here and there and your life is spiraling out of control. Slow down, lean in to your spirit, live in the moment, savor each happening, and empty your mind and soul of the noise. Your soul is trying to get your attention for your sake and for your kids' sake.

God's Signals

We really do hear God's voice; we really do get messages from Him. He will not let our children fall too far without giving us signals to recalibrate our attention to them. But we cannot hear the messages if there is too much background noise going on in our lives and in our heads. Take time to empty your brain of distracting thoughts, spend quiet time nourishing your spirit, live in the moment of one thing at a time, and you will surely hear the Creator's voice! He will direct you.

And please, do set rules with regard to your children's screen time and social media. Any laptop usage should occur in the presence of adults. With cell phones, please make sure you discuss limitations with the level of access your kids have to various apps and sites. Check the phones occasionally to make sure they are following the rules, and ensure that all their devices are brought to a safe place— like your bedroom—before their bedtimes (otherwise the kids will stay up all night surfing the web!). If you do, they learn to put their devices away and to acknowledge and enjoy the presence of other people around them.

Have gentle consequences in place for the breaking of rules. Children thrive with order and routines (not with disorganization and no boundaries!). Teach your children that human-to-human interactions are still the best, most fulfilling way.

Raising and nurturing children takes a lot of commitment. As balanced, stable, and steadfast adults, we can accomplish the successful upbringing of our children! Our children are precious. They deserve only the best, and they are the hope for a bright future.

You can tell by now that I have a deep-seated passion for the well-being of our kids. It's no coincidence that my full first name, *Iyabode,* means *the mother has come back*, and that my primary career is as a pediatrician! And now here I am, writing books to spread the word.

Kids are our seeds for a brighter, united, and peaceful future.

Chapter 4

Our Relationships

Love yourself intensely first. Accept and honor yourself first, and then you will find someone who will love, accept, and honor you.

For those who may be wondering if I'm capable of helping you make the best decisions in choosing a life partner since my own marriage turned out not to be with someone who empowered and supported me, let me write this: if you continue to read this book with a heart that is wide open, this book will change your relationship life in a healthy, empowering, and positive way.

Let's begin by discussing the relationships we hold with our friends though, and not our spouses or lovers. I'm choosing friends because every single one of us has them.

The Beauty of Friendship

Friends are an essential part of our lives. We form friendships in preschool and elementary school; in middle school, high school, and college; in our neighborhoods and through our workplaces; during leisure activities and interests; and in our later years during our new daily routines. These friendships often transform us in significant ways. Our friends can be crucial to our physical and spiritual lines, although this influence can either be positive or a negative.

I have an important message: Having and keeping a friend should be effortless. True friendships are easy. They are enjoyable, empowering, and fun, and we miss being with our true friends when they are not around us.

Friendships differ on the spectrum of closeness. Some friends are very close ones, and these are the individuals who will know a lot, or perhaps almost everything, about our lives. Others may just be acquaintances, and so we pick and choose our confidences with them.

However, no matter how close the friend is to you (or not), the relationship must still be *balanced*. In other words, each of you must equally know what's going on in each other's lives. It must balance out. A friend is someone who will be there for you during bumpy times when you are struggling and who will also be there to share and celebrate your successes. The reverse is also true: you must be there for them during those kinds of times. This type of give-and-take friendship is *balanced*.

Dysfunctional Friendships

If you notice that what you are discussing with your friend most of the time is you, your life, your struggles and successes, and all the questions and advice are centered around you, and you haven't heard anything about their life in months or in forever—the relationship is *unbalanced*. You may also have friendships in which the other person is inquisitive about your life but does not share anything personal about their life. If you ask that person about how their life is going and they clam up and change the subject, you will need to make some changes.

When you know nothing, or very little, about a friend's life, with the main topic of discussion always revolving about your life, this friendship is *dysfunctional*. Or if you are always having to listen only to their problems and can never get a word in, and all discussions revolve around them, this too is a dysfunctional friendship. The discussion cannot and should not remain one sided.

In discussing dysfunctional friendships, please notice I did not write earlier you *may* need to make changes. No, what I wrote was that you *will* need to make some changes. If the one-sidedness has been ongoing for a period of time, it will affect the friendship negatively, ultimately leading to envy, jealousy, resentment, and bad energy. Fortunately, the changes you'll have to make do not require a complete breakup of that friendship. What you may need is to change your communication level courteously and with love.

Sharing a life in a friendship must occur at the same level. There must be an almost equal back-and-forth going on. Otherwise, it is not a true, authentic relationship.

Now, this rule doesn't apply in situations where the other person is going through a major acute life situation that needs your intense help; for example, a death in their family; a sudden, perhaps chronic, illness (or any kind of illness, really); sudden financial trouble; a divorce; and other major life-threatening situations. During such situations, give wisely and reasonably! *Pour into your friend without expecting anything in return. You must do what you can, within your capability, to lift that person back up.* But in day-to-day life where no one is undergoing something traumatic or threatening, the friendship should be one of give-and-take.

Does what I've just written seem selfish? Are you wondering, Why should I expect something in return? Isn't it better to just give and be kind? To be nice to others and listen to their stories, or to open up to them if that's what they are looking for, because it makes them feel good?

Of course you should be kind and nice, but if your friend is not giving back equally to you, eventually this relationship will drain you of many good feelings! Resentment and negative energy will build up within you, and the friendship will end badly. This is because we all have the hope that we will get something from our friendships. We all hope to build our friends up, and we hope they build us up too.

That's really what friendships—in fact, all relationships—are about: They are about caring for those persons and making their lives better and more wholesome—something you surely expect they will do and feel for you! If it is not a mutual give-and-receive, it is not a true friendship.

Can This Relationship Be Fixed?

In some relationships that are not working, you both can decide to talk about your needs and express yourselves about any ongoing friendship issues, such as if you are not feeling the friendship in return. Then you can discuss what you can both do to make changes. But this only works sometimes, mostly commonly in closer, long-term relationships like marriage and others that have a deep commitment and two balanced people. It does not always work in all "regular" friendships.

If you choose to talk with a friend to whom you are not very close, or who is usually on the defensive, and you tell that person you feel they are "just taking from you on all levels," and you don't feel you are getting anything in return, it may backfire. They may think you are being needy and too sensitive—and once they express such sentiments, the relationship may spiral out of control. So I caution you to use judgment in terms of which of your friends you should sit down with to discuss any negative concerns about the relationship. Trust your gut. If you sense talking to your friend about trying to balance the give-and-take equally will backfire, don't do it. Your best option here is to decide to slowly, temporarily or permanently, phase them out of your life. Consciously dropping things (a friendship) you've had in your life for a long time, and which has been part and parcel of your life, can be tough. But do not be worried about doing this. As long as it is done with love, and in a mature, gracious manner, it is okay.

So this is what you must do—*with love and dignity*, I emphasize. Do not gossip about the person to other friends. Do not call them to tell them off, or yell at them to let them know how disappointed you are in them. Be mature and somewhat objective, and acknowledge that not everything goes the way you hope or plan for and that it is okay to bow out of some life situations with grace.

How do you go about doing so? *Slowly reduce the amount of phone calls and text messages*, for example, as well as the physical interactions. For example, if you have been calling that person four days a week, dial it back. Call three days a week, and then reduce the frequency to two. Or if they often are the ones calling you, *do not answer every time they call.* For those times when you do answer, be kind, polite…and somewhat brief. If you continue doing this, they will eventually get the message and reduce their contact with you. If they are not getting the message, you will have to let them know directly that you don't think the friendship is working and you would like to take a break.

Never feel guilty about bowing out of friendships that are not good for you. Trying to hold on to negative energy and suboptimal influences chips away at your spiritual lifeline and knocks you off balance in terms of proceeding steadily in a forward motion.

You are the only one responsible for keeping your spiritual and physical lines in tune. If you are having a bumpy ride with a friendship, and you've given it time to change but the bumps are only getting bumpier, you must make a change: it's for the good of your life! You cannot expect another party to enact the kind of change that is necessary for *you*. They are in the middle of their own lines and trying to make their own life work, but chances are they do not hold the same knowledge and awareness you do! Of course, you can hope they will get the flow of their lines back to straight. But your focus is on *yourself* and what *you* have to do to nourish your lines and keep yourself upright in forward motion.

If anyone is preventing you from living by the fruit of the spirit as you pursue peace, you must make changes *for yourself*. You have absolutely no responsibility in terms of making someone else change.

If you try to pressure another into changing, he or she may buckle under the pressure and change for you at first, but over time resentment will build up in both parties and things will spiral out of control. When it does, and it surely will, *make the decision in your own heart to reduce contact with that person, start straightening your bumpy lines back out, and proceed in forward motion.* Reduce or stop contact with this person, and do it with love and absolutely no resentment against them.

That's right: You must walk away with *absolutely no angst or negative feelings about that person.* Otherwise you are still not living by the fruit of the spirit. You will not get back into the process of pursuing peace if you continuously blame her or him or blame yourself for a failed friendship.

Remember, quality over quantity: it is not the number of friends you have in your "collection," but their quality.

In order to straighten out your lines, if you have to let go of someone who was your *only* friend, work on making another friend. There are people everywhere, and there's absolutely no point in keeping an unbalanced friendship because of sentiments like, "But we've been friends since elementary school," or, "I just don't want to hurt anyone!"

When a friendship is slowly causing major bumps in your lines and pulling you away from focusing on the pursuit of peace, you are wasting your time. And your time is *precious*. You are delaying the peace process. End relationships without fear, guilt, or obligation so that you can both accept the change in a positive way and move ahead with your lives.

Three Chances!

Notice I suggested earlier that you could let go of some friendships temporarily. Well, I wrote that because life gives us second, third, fourth, and fifth chances. Actually no, let's keep it to three chances: if a person needs a *fifth* chance to get back on track, they require a professional to help them sort out their obviously deep-seated issues.

So yes, you can let go of a friendship temporarily and revisit it again *up to three times* to try to make it work. After all, no one is perfect. We aren't either, and so we must give each other chances. But don't rush back in after a time apart; ease back in slowly, with caution. Gauge their response, analyze their demeanor, and slowly figure out if they have been working on their individual lines. If, during your time apart, both of you were working on your lines, your friendship will work when given this new opportunity, and it could potentially become the best it has ever been!

Relationships Matter, Not Someone's Particular Religion

Relationships are a vital part of our parallel physical and spiritual lines. Human interactions can make us…or break us. We live our lives from the day we are born with people around us everywhere, and we must interact with them. If we focus more on how to make, sustain, and nourish our human-to-human relationships, our lives would be so much better. It would become so much easier for us to pursue and experience peace.

We spend so much energy trying to condemn people who are not "religious" in the same way we are, and we judge the religions that differ from our own. We fail to spend enough time teaching people how to live by the simple fruit of the spirit, nurture their human interactions, and find and keep pursuing that ultimate state of peace.

Relationships matter, and someone's particular religion does not! Religions only exist to teach us how to get better at relationships with other humans and with God.

If we existed alone, and there was no one else around, we would not need religion. The teaching of religion is fundamentally aimed at improving all our relationships. Themes of the heart, and how we use heart issues to make the world a better place, matter the most.

We all know the bottom line: Love your neighbor as yourself. Live by the fruit of the spirit in all your human interactions.

Romantic Relationships

So now, we are moving on to talk about the other kind of relationship…the romantic type (whether it involves a husband, wife, boyfriend, girlfriend, or any other kind of romantic life partner). So boys and girls from age sixteen to a hundred and ten, please listen: This is one of those really important ladybug moments. A spiritual, deep-down-in-our-souls moment.

Your upbringing and childhood influence the shape of your future relationships. To explain this fully, I'll rewind back to my own childhood.

I was blessed and lucky to have been brought up by awesome parents who had an amazing relationship with each other. My parents were together from when they were very young in their adult life, and they enjoyed a balanced relationship. Both had their individual businesses and career paths too. My mum owned her own business, a shop where she sold ethnic fabrics and jewelry. My dad had his own business in construction and real estate. They also invested in real estate together.

Socially, my parents went out to a lot of parties. But they also enjoyed social lives that were completely independent of one another. For example, my mum and her older sister often dressed up and went out to events by themselves. As for Dad, he met up with friends in his social club on the weekends. This social lifestyle pattern, both independent and mutual, worked for them because there was love, trust, and security flowing between my dad and my mum. Their union worked, and my parents lived and enjoyed a balanced relationship. They were fulfilling and nourishing their own independent lifelines, and so their lives when combined also worked.

While my parents exhibited a balanced relationship, it was, of course, not perfect. (There are no perfect relationships, and you already know how I feel about the word "perfect!") But I knew my dad loved my mum dearly, and she loved him too. My dad expressed his love in many ways. One of my favorites was seeing my dad serving my mum tea and biscuits. While some men would never imagine themselves getting up and walking up a set of stairs just to make a cup of tea for their wives, my dad would walk up and down three levels of stairs in my Atlanta townhome several times a day to get different items from the kitchen for his wife. I am well aware some men are taught to believe serving their wives or girlfriends in this kind of manner means they are not exhibiting masculine behavior. *News flash: There is nothing weak about this type of man! A man who does this is actually very secure and strong. This type of man loves his wife dearly and is not afraid or insecure to show it.*

So this is the kind of love I saw in my parents' relationship as a kid. And guess what? I subconsciously assumed I would have a marriage like this, and I planned on enjoying a marriage like this!

Sadly, this is something I thought would happen automatically once I got married. I was not in tune with, and did not fully grasp at the time, the notion that marriage between two people who come from different backgrounds could be challenging, and each partner could have had varied experiences and influences that would lead to a different expectation of marriage. Not necessarily wrong or right, just different.

But enough on that for now… Let's focus on when a relationship between two people who love each other is in balance.

Magic in a Marriage

Magic happens when two people who have been individually nourishing their lines come together and decide to commit to a relationship or a lifetime together. They remain united in peace, even when life starts to throw its inevitable curveballs and bends and bumps. They stand together in forward motion and know exactly how to work through those times and get back on the smoothly flowing peace process again.

But if only one of them (or neither) is nourishing their lines, things get rocky, and the relationship may give. Unions and marriages only work if there are two balanced people involved. Not perfect people, just balanced and wholesome people. These are people who know that they have to continuously pursue peace by nourishing their two lifelines.

For love/romantic relationships to work, we each must work on pursuing our own state of permanent happiness first—our own *individual* peace process. This will lead to balance in your life, and then you can clearly determine the kind of person who deserves you: someone balanced who is continuously working on their own lifelines. A person who has worked on fostering a peaceful, permanently happy disposition by working on their spiritual and physical lines will not settle for someone who is not working on their peace process as well. It just never happens.

Time for a Time-Out

If you are twisting and turning in the middle of your lines (curved lines), you do not have clarity as to what you truly want in life. **It is impossible to figure out the kind of person you want to spend the rest of your life with if you have not embarked on the process of figuring out who you are yourself, or the direction you want your life to go.**

Imagine being in the middle of your lines, and you keep looking at past hurts when you should be moving forward. Or what about if you are confused about what you want to do in life, have just lost your job for some reason, are struggling with financial issues, are dealing with self-esteem or body-image issues, struggling with drug addictions, or are totally confused as to why a recent love relationship failed? You are obviously experiencing a lot of bumps, twists, and humps...*and if you try to embark on a love relationship while in this state, you will fail.*

Think about this: if you were to make a list of what you are looking for in a partner when in this state, it would be misguided and unrealistic! All you would be seeking is someone to rescue you from your sadness, your apathy, and your problems! However, no one else can do this for you—*only you can!* Believe me when I inform you that you will have to take a time-out from intimacy to get your lines back to a steady forward motion before you can embark on and enjoy a successful relationship. You must have an authentic, true relationship with your inner soul before you can successfully merge your soul with someone else's.

Reminder: *You are alone when you are in between your lines.* No one can "bail you out" of there! You must recognize the unsteady state of your lines and do all you can to get yourself back on track first before pulling someone else into your life.

For those of you to whom this applies:

1. Stop looking to find a life partner for the wrong reasons.

2. Stop getting married for the wrong reasons.

3. Stop staying too long in disordered marriages.

There is no man or woman in this world who can take on the responsibility for supplying you with everything you need for permanent happiness and peace. Of course they can love you and care for you with all their hearts, but it is you, and you alone, who are solely responsible for your own happiness and peace. Make peace with yourself. If you find peace with yourself, then you will be able to pick a like-minded person, and not just any Tom, Dick, or Harry, or in fact any Mary, Jane, or Jill, you think is good for you (but who is actually not). This is so important, and I am hoping everyone is tuning in closely here.

Finding Peace and True Love

Once we are moving forward in between our lines and pursuing peace, it is extremely empowering and insightful to make a list of what we are looking for in a love partner. Writing down your true desires and reading them aloud to yourself afterward helps you recognize whether the wishes are right and true.

As you read them aloud and decide whether or not to affirm them, you will be able to distinguish ones that resonate with your inner soul, then cross off unrealistic ones that aren't harmonious.

Ignite the Fire!

It is easy to lodge misguided, grandiose, and unrealistic hopes and thoughts in the deepest parts of our souls where we keep them secret from our conscious selves. Isn't that funny? We keep secrets from our own selves! We wish for things we know are not right, things we know are not good for us, but because we do not ever write them down and thus consciously acknowledge and analyze them, we keep on living a life where we are wishing for, and moving toward, the wrong goals. As we do this, we keep believing in them in our very hearts and souls.

To extinguish this, let's put into practice the simple act of compiling a goal list for all aspects of our lives. Make lists of all the goals and the hopes that we have—not only for love and relationships but for work and other parts of our lives.

There's something so powerful about writing down our thoughts, for as we write them down clearly, it ignites the fire of sensible thinking inside of us and immediately cancels out the unrealistic, grandiose, and/or negative expectations we have of life. It's like we are no longer keeping a secret from ourselves anymore and have stopped being selfish to our own selves. We are telling ourselves the truth now!

Journaling, wherein we write down our goals and dreams, is a must-do as we pursue peace. Please trust me on this. It works! I personally have journaled my way to great and peaceful outcomes in every area and stage of my life.

So let's think about some things you may write down. For example, "I plan to complete my college education in the next three years, then get a paying job in a top firm for the next two years before I leave to pursue a master's degree. After that I desire to open my own business, then meet and marry a really nice person. I want to have three kids and live in a nice part of town." Well, I believe these are realistic and healthy goals!

A piece of advice, though: as you write down and identify your objectives and dreams, then start to act and work toward them, surround yourself with positive people. They will help you along the way—and you will achieve your goals!

But here's a very different example of what a person might write down: Let's say you are a twenty-three-year-old college dropout who abandoned your education because of not wanting to study, and you write down, "I am no longer going to bother pursuing an education. Instead, my goal is to find a wealthy spouse to take care of me so I can stay at home and never have to work again." Well, I am confident that as you write this down, you might reconsider your plan in the light of day! You might suddenly think, *Wow, is this really my main objective in life? Do I really want to be beholden to someone else in this way? Besides, what will inspire me when I am at home all the time? What interests should I pursue? Well, if I want someone to marry me, maybe I should work on my education so that I am more informed on a lot of issues and can converse on a higher level with them. And if I'm home all alone every day with not that much to do because my partner is paying for it all, maybe I might end up wanting to work because it might get boring after a time!*

When we blindly follow unrealistic or misguided hopes and dreams, we make big, damaging, often irreversible mistakes in life. However, if we come to identify and analyze these hopes and goals because we write them all down, we tend to correct them and revise them to more realistic, attainable, and positive goals.

Writing down your goals immediately helps you refrain from lying to yourself. People who practice journaling and affirmations are more realistic, balanced people and do much better in life.

So stop keeping secrets from yourself, the things that are hidden away somewhere inside of you, eating away at you slowly and denying you peace. Identify and write your goals down, then cross off and delete the unrealistic or grandiose hopes permanently. *Replace them with balanced goals, true reality, and obvious truths.*

Affirm the truths always.

The Beauty and Power of Lists

If you are looking for something but don't know what it is you are looking for, you will never find it! So making lists is essential to truly pursue peace and permanent happiness.

Lists make the directions we are going to take clear. They keep us focused and organized so that we can strive after and reach our dreams. Journaling / writing our goals / making lists is a powerful and vital tool in maintaining a balanced life.

Why are *vision boards* so popular these days? (*Vision* or *dream boards* are collages of pictures, affirmations, and desires that inspire and motivate people to achieve their goals.) For the very reason that as soon as you write your goals down with supporting pictures, and you affirm and believe in them, you are on your way to living and achieving your hopes and dreams!

Once you have made a realistic list of what you are looking for in a romantic partner, you must *stick to it.* Do not give excuses for yourself, or for your love interest, for behavior that is unacceptable. Do not get carried away in the heat of the moment or by lust. Do not ever lower your standards. If you do, this will backfire and come back to haunt you.

Time to Date!

Once you're in a steady forward motion as a result of working on and maintaining your spiritual and physical lines, and after you've written down the goals and qualities you are looking for in a partner, it is time to start dating. First, though, a word about appearance, both for the gals *and* the guys.

Ladies, please dress tastefully—like a lady. One thing that means is you need to *leave something to the imagination!* If your boobs are hanging out or you are wearing a dress so tight that you look naked to most people, you will attract the wrong kind of guys and repel the good ones. No mature, wise, and steadfast guy in the world will be proud to show you off to his friends and family and have you beside him if you dress too provocatively. Instead, clothe yourself in a sophisticated, tasteful, and classy, yet still sexy, way. Doing so will boost your self-confidence—and attract the right guys into your life.

Men (and women) can't get to know someone really well if they are completely distracted by the other person dressing in a flashy way. What well might happen then is that they may end up focusing entirely on the physical, to the exclusion of the person's other wonderful qualities. And while physical attraction is of course important, it is not *the* most important factor. Of course we must feel attracted to our dates, but we must go beyond the physical to see what they have in their souls. While we see the physical first before we get to know the person well, and this is what will initially attract us, everyone likes a tastefully dressed person.

Gentlemen, the same applies to you… Please dress appropriately. For example, please pull up any low-hanging pants. We don't enjoy seeing your underwear (except for when you are showing it off to your romantic partner behind closed doors). Dress like a gentleman so you can attract the right kind of women into your life. You do not have to be decked out in a jacket and tie if you are going to a place that sports a casual atmosphere, but a black shirt tucked into a pair of jeans can look sexy and appealing to many ladies.

If you're not sure *what* to wear and don't have any good role models to advise and critique you on your dressing, go online and Google "what to wear on a date." Doing so will help you discover how to put together a nice outfit from pieces you already own without having to buy new clothes. If you're used to dressing in a flashy way all the time, you should overhaul the way you dress every day and not only when you go out on dates. No serious, steadfast, loyal person in life will take you seriously if you dress in a reckless and distasteful manner. You cannot attract a quality love partner if you are not displaying that you are a quality person yourself!

Also make sure you are keeping yourself in good shape by eating balanced and healthy meals and maintaining a good physical activity routine, in order to keep your self-esteem high. You cannot attract quality people if you have low self-esteem. And when you are unhappy with your weight or appearance, it makes you insecure. Insecurity ruins relationships. So please work on achieving a healthier diet and exercising regularly.

How do you get asked out? These days people meet online on dating sites; get introduced by friends; meet each other at events and activities; strike up conversations when out shopping, taking classes, or taking a flight—doing just about anything outside of your home provides an opportunity for a date!

After you have agreed to go on a first date, please remember this: *Do not have expectations. That person is not yet your spouse.* Simply relax and attempt to have as much fun as you can. (By "fun," I mean being in tune with yourself while you get to know the other person. I am not referring to sex, drinking heavily, or acting wild and crazy.)

Also, please do not sleep with a stranger on the first few dates. This is wrong and unsafe on so many levels. Do not drink too much alcohol—avoid getting tipsy or drunk.

All the Single Ladies!

A bit of special advice for all my female readers out there interested in dating… Do not be overtly sexual on the first few dates. Just be a lady, and own your femininity in a classy way.

When you arrive at the date, say hello and give your date a hug, and then after the initial greeting just smile and act comfortably and confidently. Let the guy start to initiate questions. *Please be aware that this is the only situation I discuss in this book where I ask my female readers not to be "doers."*

The point I am making here is that you don't need to control everything about the date. Just "being" in this situation is much better than "doing." So…do not start the date by asking him a "laundry list" of questions! There is no way you will get to know him if you rattle off question after question—you will just come across as a nervous, needy, and insecure wreck. Your anxious questions will turn him off.

Remember, it's not a job interview; it's a date. Sure you should ask him a few questions that are important to you, but keep them light: no questions about income, the type of car he drives, or why his marriage failed. And if you ask him one question for every three to four questions he asks you, soon enough you will get a good feel for what he is like. So relax, have fun, and listen to everything he tells you, because for sure he will tell you a lot about himself. He will reveal to you most of what you need to know even on that very first date!

The other thing you have to remember is: don't be crushed if he never wants to see you again after the date! After all, you are not the only one trying to determine if you two will make good partners. He has a choice to make too, and his decision may differ from yours.

After the date, let *him* text you or call you first to thank you and or ask you out again. A man who is interested in you will contact you again.

He did not lose your number.

He was not in a car accident.

He did not fall, hit his head, and lose his memory.

Nor is he afraid of calling you. He knows perfectly well if he wants to see you again or not. You need to wait it out and get busy doing other things that are fulfilling. Meet other guys; go out on other dates. Take your mind off him! If he does not contact you, let it go. He was not "the one."

If it is the other way around and he contacts you but you did not like him and do not want to see him again, please let him know *politely*. Don't just ignore all his attempts to reach you; that is rude and not kind. Please respond and let him know you enjoyed the date with him, but you don't feel you are a good match, and you sincerely wish him the best. If you absolutely know you don't want to see him again, and there was no connection whatsoever, you must let him know in a kind, polite way.

If you are not sure how you feel about him, go out with him again until you gain clarity. It's perfectly okay to date just one guy at a time, as long as you are not hyperfocused on him and looking for a wedding dress on date three because you are sure he loves you and you love him. Take it slow. Take time to get to know him. And do not have sex with him until you've discussed exclusivity. Practice safe sex on all levels.

Some of you may raise an eyebrow when you read this bit of advice, but it is *okay* to date more than one guy at once for a while—for several weeks to a few months—if you are trying to make a decision. However, you cannot have sex with any of these guys during this time. Sleeping with them will completely ruin your level of clarity about who is your best "fit," and you will not be able to make an informed, intelligent choice. It is also unsafe, as you have not committed to any of them. If you and your dates are sleeping around a bit, you open yourself to the risk of a sexually transmitted disease and other dangers.

As for why I wrote that it is okay to date more than one gentleman at a time—it takes time to get to know someone. There is nothing wrong with getting to know more than one guy at a time, so long as you are comfortable with it. However, this is not for everyone. If you would rather not, that's fine too!

A Guy Can't Make You Happy

This section is particularly for young ladies, from the dating age of sixteen or so all the way to middle aged (and even older) who are dating. Listen in, please: *A guy cannot "make" you happy.* He cannot. Your chosen life partner is not responsible for your joy and inner peace and fulfillment. You are solely responsible for this. Your partner/spouse is not there to support you through all life's circumstances and provide all your needs—for example, money, joy, and material, emotional, and spiritual needs.

As for those single women who are on the prowl for a rich, handsome, educated, and successful guy to pick them up and supply all their life needs. If this is your goal, you will be badly hurt, maybe even to the point of irreversible hurt. No one, and no one man, can "pick you up." Only you, yourself, can "pick you up." So what should you do? Work on getting a great education so that you can land and keep a job you are passionate about. Work on keeping your spiritual and physical lines steady and moving forward. Discover what your gifts and talents are, and use them for your good and the good of others first. Then you can attract that guy I just described.

If you love yourself intensely first—if you accept and honor yourself first—then you *will* find someone who will love, accept, and honor you! So look in the mirror, and appreciate what you see in it. Break out in song and dance in honor of the beautiful woman you see reflected there. Then, when you go out, dress like a lady, put those heels on, and *strut your stuff!*

If you've dropped out of school in tenth grade, or quit your job because your boss was a bad person, or just don't see the reason why you should get an education or a job if a man can provide that for you, and now you feel lazy and hopeless and are sitting around doing nothing, or have a minimum-wage job and no plan to go for a better job, but think that because you are the prettiest, sexiest girl on the block who dresses provocatively and gets wolf whistles and head turns, that you can capture that rich, wealthy, successful guy, think again. (Sorry, but I had to get all that into one long sentence!) *You are heading for disaster. That marriage or union will not work.* You may think you are lucky if you meet up with a rich, wealthy, successful, but deeply insecure guy who seeks out girls in a much-lower economic and emotional rank than him, but the pairing will not work. That pairing only makes for a dysfunctional relationship. He will never see your value, and he will mistreat you—and you will come to feel trapped and insecure. It's a lose-lose situation.

Please recognize I'm not implying a wealthy guy cannot be compatible with and date a lady who is not as successful as him. What I am revealing is that each person, individually, has to work on her or his own physical and spiritual sustenance. *No one else can help us do that, not even our lovers or spouses.*

So if I've just shot your dating plan to pieces…what should you do instead? Try to answer the following questions as you look at your reflection in the mirror:

- Who am I?

- What would I like to do or achieve in my life?

- What would I like my future to look like?

- What's important to me in life?

- What would make me wake up happy and peaceful every morning?

As you ask and answer the questions out loud, affirm and believe in them—and proceed to visualize everything for which you are hoping! But don't put too much pressure on yourself: it may take some time to get all the answers figured out. However, if some answers do come quickly as you ask yourself these questions, say those answers out loud as you look in the mirror. If some come to you later on, write them down in your journal. Then repeat the practice of affirmations every day while looking in the mirror.

By the way…I absolutely refuse to believe that any female reader will say out loud, while looking at her reflection in the mirror, something like, "I am Iyabo Ojikutu, a confident, beautiful lady. I would like to meet a man who will provide for me in every way and take care of me so that I won't have to get an education or work a day in my life. I would like him to be totally responsible for my keep, my happiness, and my joy. I really don't want to achieve anything of my own; I just want him to be there for me, to love me, and to provide for me. I would like to have a happy future with him, including maybe three kids, and I want all of us to be happy. It is important to me that my husband is very wealthy, buys me a lot of material things, and is always there for me. In fact, I'm hoping he can buy me that brand-new car and those designer shoes and bags I've been eyeing. It would be great if he could take me to Bora Bora one day. Those are my future goals, and this is what I am hoping for. I'm beautiful physically, so I deserve a guy who has all those qualities and can get me all that!"

Well, my fellow ladies, I am placing a bet (and I don't bet!) that none of us will ever look at ourselves in the mirror and affirm all this. When you say such things out loud, you realize how bad, unrealistic, shallow, and foolish they sound.

However, while I can guarantee none of us ladies will say this out loud or write it down in our journals, the reality is some actually do believe in this dysfunctional set of wishes that we have tucked secretly away in the deepest parts of our souls! We then start to seek this magical (and by *magical* I mean *not realistic*) man of our dreams who will supply our every need. But if we have to say such wishes out loud as we stare at our reflections in the mirror or as we write them down in our journals, it makes us acknowledge how unrealistic we are being! And this can be the very reason why a lot of us do not enjoy journaling or making lists of our goals in life: as we identify our inner, hidden goals and write them down, we can realize how disconnected, unrealistic, shallow, and selfish we are being to ourselves.

We are being selfish to our own selves if we are hiding the truth about what we want from ourselves. We actually know what is right, realistic, and true for our life goals, but if we have tucked a bunch of lies and misguided hopes and dreams away in our souls, we then act on them, seeking out their manifestations. This is a waste of our time. We are prolonging and delaying the manifestation of our potentially awesome lives by upholding unrealistic expectations that we lie to ourselves about!

Why Others Want Us

We all must start to be more true to ourselves and begin teaching ourselves (and our kids, if we have them) to voice and write down our life visions and dreams often. (Kids and teens should do this from an early age and may need to modify it as they get older. For example, they can write down goals for a few years at a time, then adjust it from time to time as they get more in touch with their hopes and dreams.)

Each person must work on himself or herself first and be the person a good partner would want to live the rest of their life with, rather than focus on what someone else can do to help enrich, mold, and support your life. Remember, we are *alone* in the middle of our spiritual and physical lines, and so we are responsible to *individually* sustain our own lines so that we are individuals pursuing peace, fully enriching our lives, and living in peace. If we are…we will attract a like-minded person with strong values and a good moral center.

All the Single Men!

The same rules apply to men: they must teach themselves (and adults must teach their young sons) to support and nourish their spiritual and physical lines and to live by the fruit of the spirit. If they do, they make themselves into the men with whom ladies want to spend the rest of their lives.

When men practice the heart issues—the fruit of the spirit—they are well balanced, loyal, and steadfast. A good man is strong but humble; gentle, patient, and kind; and loves his partner unconditionally. A good man does want to take care of his woman, of course, but he does not want a needy woman who is totally dependent on him. (That kind of woman gets "old" quickly.)

Tuning In to Others

As you date, be in tune with your instincts. If you are keeping your physical and spiritual lines flowing steadily while in the dating process, and having your quiet time, praying or getting in tune with your spirit, you will have a clear sense of who is right for you. But that's not all you need: *you must also find one to three trustworthy people to help you to make a decision about your potential partner.* Notice I wrote "trustworthy"—limit the amount of people whose advice you should listen to about your date. Listening to the advice of any number of people greater than three becomes "noise" and no longer solid advice.

Choosing one to three trustworthy individuals is almost as important as finding this life partner you are looking for. You require mature, nonjudgmental, nonenvious, steadfast, and balanced individuals in your life who have shown you in the past that they have your back and will give you real, heartfelt insight and advice. Explain to them what you want your potential partner to be like, and discuss the qualities you have written down. Open up completely to them, and let them give you honest insight into what they think about your desires, your potential partner, and your dating experiences. Now, since you took the time to select these individuals based on your trust level for them, you must also take the time to listen as they give you their advice, and take it very seriously.

This is important for *all* age groups! If you are younger and you've been dating someone you are starting to like, please look for mature, wiser individuals to give you a clear insight about that person. This is so important. Your mom or dad can be this person; so can older siblings, an aunt or uncle, or another mentor or coach whom you admire and trust. Please take their insights seriously, and do not give excuses or twist around what they've told you to suit your short-term needs. You must seriously consider their opinions, for the people closest to you see what you yourself don't see.

When I was seventeen, my close friends and family gave me their opinions about whom I started to date, but I chose not to listen. **They saw what I did not see, and the very thing they all saw was the very situation that eventually caused me a lot of unrest and ups-and-downs in my marriage.** All of us have loved ones who want the best for us! Listen to them, and ponder their advice.

If you feel you don't have any family or friends whose opinion you can trust, look for a lifestyle coach, or perhaps ask your hairdresser or barber. There *has* to be someone trustworthy in your life whom you can approach. So go "out of the box" and brainstorm who that person might be!

Too, if you have more than one person giving you the same kind of advice—and these people don't even know each other—you had best be wise about taking it seriously.

Red Flags

When a person you date shows you certain signs about herself or himself, believe in the signs. You know the qualities you are looking for, and if you've met someone who lacks any of your deal-breaker qualities—or has one or several red flags—please take these seriously and do not waste your time hoping they will change or that you can change the person. *No one changes for anyone. People only change for themselves, and only when they are ready.* As Oprah once said, "If people show you who they are, believe them immediately."

Don't waste time. Time is precious.

When I started to date after my divorce, I compiled a list of my absolute deal-breakers in a relationship. But things are never that black and white, and I still encountered some situations I did not have on my list that I had to carefully ponder and discuss with those whom I trusted.

Here are two quick examples. I don't like to drive. I did drive while I lived in England and New York, but when I moved to Atlanta, I got intimidated by the large highways and slowly weaned myself off driving anywhere. I started to take taxis and limos (and now Uber) everywhere. Well, I met a guy I was starting to like, and on our tenth date or so, I decided to tell him I did not drive much anymore. He did not receive this well; I could immediately tell from the expression on his face. Well, he started to withdraw after that day, and I just knew what was going on. When I asked, he admitted the "driving issue" was a problem for him…and that's when I knew our relationship would not work. I liked him a lot, but I had to let him go. He was obviously not after my heart but was more into superficial issues. *How does a lack of driving determine who I am?* It has not prevented me from being what I am today, and it never will. It is just one of those things I am not good at and that I do not enjoy. It does not define me or prevent me from living out my life purpose. So that's how I knew he was not my match, and I moved on.

I'll give another example to further emphasize this point. Another date who was attractive and fun to be around told me on our third date that he had a concealed gun on him; he always carries one around to protect himself and whomever he is with just in case there is a mass shooting. Well, this really scared me. I did not grow up around guns, and I was terrified when he told me he had one. Needless to say, I could no longer keep seeing this guy, and our third date was the last time I saw him. I could not feel safe around a guy who carries a gun everywhere with him. *Even on dates? A bit much for me.* I know it would not bother many other women who understand the concept of guns and even enjoy guns themselves, but it just was wrong for me.

So the point here is, we must be in tune with what we are being told and what we are hearing when we are dating. People will reveal themselves to you, and it is up to you to believe them and make a wise decision to move on if you are not comfortable with what you see or hear. You trying to convince them to change will not work. It's also a waste of your time waiting around to see if they will change.

Listen to God's voice and His whispers. Do not ignore Him and then have to face the hard consequences of doing so later on.

However, there are people who may *want* to change, and if you are dating one, here's how they will act: They usually will quickly express their willingness to work on the change if it will make you happy. They will gladly volunteer—and that's how you know if they genuinely will make the change or not. You do not have to ask them repeatedly to change. If you have expressed your needs and standards once, a good partner will change if they really love you and want you in their life.

Believe people when they show you who they are, and stop living in a dream world. Get connected with reality, and do not lower your standards when in a relationship. Too many of us stay in chaotic relationships that upset us for way too long…

When to Stay, When to Go

Why stay with a partner who has cheated on you over and over? Why give your all to another who puts you down all the time because of their insecurities? Why let your partner live their own dreams while you stay home alone feeling apathetic, worthless, and lacking passion for anything?

If you have tried all you can and the relationship is not working for you, it is time for change. It is time to get up, let go, and let in.

You do not have forever, and time is *not* at a standstill. If you "make do" with a "half-" or "quarter-person," there will be no room for that full person heading your way when they eventually show up. And trust me: they *will* show up! You just have to trust, be really patient, work on yourself in the meantime, be your awesome self, use your gifts, and start living out your passion and purpose. It's not easy to wait it out, but waiting does pay off eventually.

Finding Your "Twin Flame"

It feels wonderful to have a soul mate / twin flame / life partner by your side sharing life with you...but it only feels wonderful if it is the right person! Don't let loneliness, neediness, temporary longings, materialism, codependency, confusion, and/or noise from too many people lead you down the wrong path. The best deserves the best. I myself am willing to wait it out until I find the right man for me. We singles must affirm the need to wait patiently until that special person shows up. In the meantime, life is good, life is going on, I am feeling awesome...and I am writing my first book!

The "Happy Homemaker" Choice

There is another important point on which I would like to shed some light: If you are in a relationship that is about to become permanent, we need to talk about the fact that some men do want their wives to stay home to take care of the kids and the home. Well, men, this is okay...with one caveat: Your partner must, in her deepest soul, actually want to do this. She must have thought it through carefully, and the decision must be hers. You must not pressure her or tempt her into accepting this if it is not something she is completely at peace with.

For the women who choose the path of staying at home while their partner serves as the breadwinner, I want them to know that I have encountered many ladies who chose this option only to become unhappy with the arrangement as the years rolled on by. Once the kids started heading off to school, resentment and regret started to slowly creep in, and many women started taking it out on their partners. Other women who made this same decision ended up feeling dejected, confused, and hopeless.

Consider this: your kids might love having you at home with them, but you also must work on your own happiness and fulfillment too. Otherwise, you defeat your purpose of being a good influence on them. Your kids will grow up fast and soon enough have their own independent lives... What then? Will you be staring out the window, wondering how you got into this state? So, ladies, please ponder and carefully make this choice of being a homemaker.

If you genuinely want to stay home indefinitely to take care of the home and children, please do so. However, you must be ready to accept the fact that after staying home and not being in the workforce for several years, it may be hard to secure the kind of job you may want, or muster up the confidence to pursue a skill or a career, if you decide to go back to work. So make sure you truly are at peace with this choice, especially if you choose to stay at home indefinitely. As you weigh the decision, don't forget every woman must have some form of independence in her life. She must have self-confidence and self-worth outside of her spouse, her kids, and the upkeep of the home.

How do you make the choice that is right for you? First, remember *you* are in charge of your own destiny. Second, take a deep breath before you examine what you really want your future to look like. Write it down or draw pictures of your future. Visualize your future life in your mind. Third, do not get derailed by the happiness and pleasure you will get from staying home, as this could be temporary. Also, do not let laziness, or a false sense of euphoria and hope, deceive you. Money and riches are not everything. Your spouse's success, wealth, and riches do not guarantee your future self-worth and your own lasting happiness.

Yes, we would all like spouses who can take care of us, but remember how we already talked about *temporary* happiness coming from *external* events, people, and influences, and *permanent* happiness coming from *internal* and personal choices? Well, we can only be permanently happy if we make internal positive choices. Otherwise, we experience short-lived, on-and-off happiness states.

Handling Your Own Destiny

We need to take care of ourselves first. *We need to own our own powers. We need to own our God-given gifts.* We were born to make use of our own gifts so we can live meaningful lives.

Do not sweep your personal gifts and talents under the rug and hide behind bringing up your kids and taking care of your husband and the home as an excuse for not fulfilling your potential. Your husband is flanked by his own lines (and hopefully nourishing them). So are your kids. And what about you?

Are you nourishing your own lifelines fully? Or are you trying to drag your spouse and kids in between your own lines? Well, they *cannot* come in there with you. It is impossible.

Have you served yourself first? Are you grabbing your own destiny? Or are you living in the shadows of others? The shadows of your spouse, kids, friends, and/or family members?

Remember, *you have power over your choices.* You. Only you can handle your own destiny. If you allow others—spouse, kids, friends, family, boss—to handle your destiny, you will never find it.

Moving Beyond a Failed Marriage

If you have made marriage a choice but then been unfortunate enough to have that marriage fail, take care not to blot out the hope and power that exist in your children for a bright future when it comes to their own relationships. Do not subconsciously or consciously ensure they experience the same adversity and failures you did. Do not transfer any pain, hopelessness, bitterness, and lack of forgiveness on to your kids.

Lack of forgiveness… Wow, that's huge. It's huge because it keeps *you* in a permanent state of bondage. It messes up *your* life. If you can't forgive, it constricts your soul, confuses you, pulls you away from the peace process, and prevents you from ever finding the true meaning to your life. That one word—*forgiveness*—holds so much power.

Please allow a forgiving heart to empower you, free you, and help you to move mountains and hurdle past all obstacles to find and embark on your pursuit of peace again. Let go of past hurts, and break free from bondage. There is no hope, chance, or possibility with the past. The future, however, holds so much hope, chances, and possibilities. Why waste the future and die wishing you had grabbed on to those opportunities? Remember, my friends, the future becomes the past so quickly. Stop wasting time, and stop holding on to past hurts and a lack of forgiveness.

If you are not forgiving and letting go of all hurt, you are *not* moving on. You may brag out loud that you have moved on, but you know, in the deepest part of your soul, you still harbor major resentment against that someone else you were involved with. You are still holding on and blaming the other person who was in your failed relationship. Well, remember, you are flanked by your own lines. You must nourish yours and work on yours so your kids can see that and experience the same.

Parents, do not tell your kids marriage is hopeless and pointless. Give your kids hope and a future instead. Just because it did not work for you does not mean it won't work for them one day. Give them all the wisdom you gleaned from your broken marriage. Give them good, loving, and thoughtful advice. Exhibit love, hope, and gentleness…and don't talk badly about another person. Be a good role model who has learned well from your past and who is now equipping your kids to choose better, do better, and experience better. Pray for your kids and support them in their choices.

Why do you think statistics show that kids from homes with failed marriages or single-parent households don't do as well in life? Kids brought up in single-parent homes do not fail because of poverty or lack of resources; they fail because of all the emotional ups-and-downs going on. Many of them have parents who are holding on to pain, fear, bitterness, and anger and who transfer all those emotions and the resulting behavior patterns onto them. The parents are gripped by fear as well: The fear of the unknown for their kids. And fear drives out love.

However, personally and professionally, I also have seen many kids from single-parent homes turn out to be great kids—emotionally stable, successful kids who are living out their purposes. This is because their single parents moved on, forgave their pasts, held on to love, kept their lifelines straight, and equipped their kids to have hope. If they were married once, they lived by the fruit of the spirit as their marriages ended, let their pasts be an essential tool for securing their futures, and started new, hopeful, bright lives. Always, they kept their gazes firmly on the future.

This can be done with the smallest, leanest, and tightest of money and resources. *Only love and hope are needed for children to thrive!* It is better for children to be brought up in an emotionally stable single-parent home than in one with two parents who are throwing objects at each other or bringing each other down with negative, abusive words every day.

Just as bad is bringing kids up in a home where neither parent speaks to each other, and each sleeps in separate bedrooms and walks past the other without making eye contact. I am also gravely concerned about the growing home model in today's world where the father is gone more than 75 percent of the time—perhaps working from a remote spot outside the home in a different location or city—and the mom takes care of virtually everything in the home, aside from maybe the money the father may provide. These parents might as well not be married, as money is not the most important factor in bringing up stable, forward-moving kids. The most important factors are *love, hope, strength,* and *boundaries* in the parents. Children see all this and take it all in. Some families live like this for way too long and damage their kids emotionally and spiritually, if not physically in some cases.

Single moms and dads, do not lead your children down the wrong paths because of what you have experienced in your relationships! They depend on you as they grow and navigate through life. We are powerful forces of influence in our kids' lives as they grow into adults. If we nurture them well in their formative years, we will not feel we have to hold on to them when they are adults.

Single Moms with Sons

I especially want to focus on the single mom-son relationship, as this one tends to be the one where there is unnecessary, unrealistic, and unhealthy codependence and attachment. So, single moms with sons, pay attention to these words: Your son cannot be the replacement for that man who hurt you, left you, and disappointed you, or the man whom you have not yet found. He cannot be your husband, boyfriend, provider, or comforter. If you have a son and you are single, you must start to nourish your own physical and spiritual lines immediately, get back out there, and find love again, no matter how old you are! Fill yourself with love, hope, joy, forgiveness, gratitude, and peace. Take care of your physical body too, and *then get out there and meet people.* You will find love again. Do not make your son your only focus in life. He must nourish his own lines by himself.

If your son is now of age, you should have already done your job of giving him the necessary tools to go out, be an adult, and make good choices, so *you must let go.* All you should do now is pray for him in your quiet times, and be there for him at the appropriate times, such as when you are truly needed. *Do not be an overbearing and needy mom!* Too, take care not to fill your son up with guilt so that he forever feels you are the only reason he is still alive! *Stop strategically reminding him of all the sacrifices you have made for him and how he would not be alive or be what he is today without you.* Don't keep him thinking that you are the be-all and end-all in his life.

Instead, teach him to love, honor, respect, and protect his wife and kids if and when he gets married. Teach him confidence, along with a good dose of humility. Teach him to be strong and courageous for his wife and kids, but please do this with a gentle and calm heart. Teach him to be hardworking and to keep a good job but to still spend daily quality time with his wife and family. Teach him the importance of nurturing his spiritual side so that he may share heart and soul issues with his wife and show his vulnerable side sometimes.

When he brings his lady home to show you off, and for you to meet her, do not be overbearing, jump to conclusions, and/or judge or envy her. Many moms despise and envy their sons' girlfriends; it's sad but true. These are the moms who have not made the conscious decision to work on their lifelines and are still living in their bitter, painful pasts. My advice to such moms is this: As long as your son's new lady is not obviously a bad decision—such as on drugs, or really crazy, or the like—please be quiet about her. Welcome them both with love, and give your son gentle, loving advice later. *Treat her the way you would like to be treated.* Besides which, I doubt that if you gave your son the right influences as you brought him up that he would come home with a less-than-desirable lady. So trust his judgment, give him your full support, exhibit love to both of them, and allow them to pursue their own peace.

If he has reached a somewhat permanent arrangement with his new partner, do not call him every second of every hour; do not make him feel guilty that he has abandoned you because he did not visit you last week; and above all, do not ask to move in with them! You should not live permanently with your child and his spouse; it seldom works.

Imagine if the spouse's parents also demanded to move in, and the new couple now has parents from both sides living with them; it's a sure recipe for disaster. Also, don't try the rationale of being a "free" nanny or babysitter to their kids because you'll be a live-in who is always there to help with your grandchildren. Nope. Sure as the crow flies, they will sort out their babysitting needs elsewhere. Or they may invite you over for a few hours of help or for a weekend if they so desire. My advice is to simply be there for them when you can, and *leave when their request has been fulfilled.* It is now your son and daughter-in-law's home, domain, and territory, so they set their own rules. It is not your territory. You've had your chance at your own marriage, and you still have more chances. Get out there and grab your chances. You can find love again at any age.

One caveat—it may work out if you live with your child and his spouse when you are very elderly and they have invited you to live with them. (Some cultures or circumstances are quite successful in doing this.) Whenever this may be, you must be invited by them—the *two* of them. The invite must arise from a mutual decision. If you are not invited, don't invite yourself and put your child and in-law in a difficult situation.

Love Can Arrive at Any Age

Hopefully, even if it's later in life, you will be busy and occupied with the love of your own life! That's my hope for all the single

91

parents out there, regardless of age: that they all have hope and grab their second chances at life and live happily ever after with their true loves.

As of this writing, I am bringing up my two teenage daughters by myself. They have been with me 99 percent of the time since my divorce. (Even before my divorce, I was the parent mostly closely involved in their daily living.) I have no residual pain, angst, or bitterness from my past that is influencing my current life with my family. You see, just like you, I had a choice: to hold on to all the disappointments from my marriage and to keep focusing on, and wishing, the other person was different, or to place my gaze and hope firmly on what I could do within my power to raise my children right.

I chose the latter because I was fully aware my internal choices were the only way to my permanent happiness fulfillment. I am so proud as I watch my daughters evolve into what God has planned for their lives. We have had our challenges, but I am confident in the solid foundation I have given them. I have instilled in them the wisdom that I have gathered so far in my life, and I know the sky is their limit. Even when the curves and bumps of life happen to them, as they surely will, my daughters will employ that solid foundation and recalibrate quickly. I trust and believe in them to make good choices. Too, I have told them I will not move in with them one day, or be an overbearing mum as they develop their own love matches. But they know I am here for them and will continue to be here for them whenever they need me, as long as God gives me breath. That is love. That is a balanced relationship.

On a final note to close this chapter on relationships and love: I have dated several men since my divorce. I've met a few good ones but just have not met the special and unique man with whom I would like to spend the rest of my life. I discuss this with my daughters. They understand I am working on myself, busy living out my life-given purpose, and having the best time of my life in my career and my new passion—writing! No doubt the special, unique guy who is deserving of me, and I of him, will soon surely show up. So my daughters know I am still seeking true love but am not lowering my standards in the meantime. They recognize they have a hopeful mum who is seeking life's true meaning, working on her lifelines, and making herself into this awesome lady that only an awesome guy will want to be with.

He will come around when the time is right.

Chapter 5

Faith and Works

Each of us has incredible power to use the gifts, the positive instruments we are born with, to magnificent and significant levels.

"I'm scared."

"I'm stressed."

"I'm broke, and I'll be broke forever! It's just too darn hard."

"I don't have an education."

"I can't."

"It takes too long."

"I'm just not good enough."

May I ask that we get rid of these thoughts before we proceed with this chapter? Let's clear our minds, hearts, and our deepest souls of all the negative thoughts before we read on.

My friends, all these thoughts are false and untrue. They are lies we tell ourselves, tricks that play with, and on, our minds. However, if we allow them to proceed unchecked, eventually they block and prevent us, sometimes permanently, from our true life experiences and fulfilling our God-given purposes! Conversely, if we dismiss these thoughts immediately when they come into our minds, we are completely transformed.

Each one of us has gifts. Every single person, from the day of their birth, is born with unique and perfect gifts, *positive instruments* or tools given to us by the creator of the universe. These precious and magnificent gifts are instantly activated as we take our first cries at birth.

The gifts that we all have are intended to inspire us as well as others and make the world a better place. Just as importantly, the effects of our positive instruments are supposed to still live on after we depart from this world.

Unfortunately, this does not always turn out to be the case. Many factors come into play and influence us as we grow up into children, young adults, and adults who prevent our God-given instruments from ever manifesting! Such factors negatively affect our two lifelines and therefore leave our gifts dormant, often permanently. What a waste of these positive tools that have so much potential but were left lying around in us and not nourished by ourselves.

Imagine a situation where you get a gift of flowers, and yet you leave those flowers on the table, never remembering to place them in a vase and water them. What happens? Slowly the flowers wither away. Yet if you had placed them in a vase, watered them daily, and ensured they had the right amount of sunlight, they would grow strong and flourish, bringing a smile to your face and to those who spied them. This is exactly how it can work with the gifts we are born with: some of us have the perfect circumstances and nourishment around us from our childhoods on to enable our gifts to grow and flourish, and some of us don't.

However, neither is bad. Let me explain. The Creator who placed the gifts in us understands that we may not nourish them right away. He understands that we may not have the right resources, people, and influences around us from an early age to help grow our gifts. So He made sure that throughout our lives we get many opportunities and reminders that our gifts are lying dormant, waiting for us to feed and nourish them in order to bring us into the fullness of our higher purposes. *We get these reminders at different times all throughout our life spans.* We also encounter different people along the way who could be instrumental in helping us bring our gifts to life, although it is up to us to notice these people and allow them into our lives.

Our Powerful Influence

Life's negativities, chaos, noise, lies, situations, and bad influences separate us and block us from using our positive instruments. These negativities come in different forms, sizes, shapes, and intensities all through our lives. A few examples of these are bad parents, absentee parents, negative and toxic relationships, generational curses, laziness, worry, envy of others, fear of failure, lack of forgiveness, false stereotypes, poor self-esteem, blaming of others, and addictive behaviors. All these are unhelpful distractions that seem to hold so much power over us but actually can be overcome by the incredible power that lies within each of our souls.

We all underestimate the power the creator of the universe has placed in us, along with His gifts to us: the positive instruments He also gave each one of us. Each person has incredible power to use those gifts we are born with to magnificent levels.

I am not suggesting we will all become president or the greatest and wealthiest CEO in the nation; the most famous doctor or attorney in town; or the best and wealthiest athlete or entertainer. I am saying we *all* have gifts that are unique and beautiful and that have the ability to touch, inspire, and bring out the best in others. The universe is a ginormous space, with people coming together and thriving by using "the division of labor" model. Some of us will be wealthy and influential, some of us will be poor and influential, and some will live a comfortable lifestyle and be influential. The common denominator is *influential*. We must all strive to be influencers.

If you are not positively influencing with the instruments given to you, you are not living. If you are not actively doing and influencing, your spirit is wasting away. The spirit within you is far more powerful than you can imagine…but you do have to nourish it.

Educate and Influence!

The word "education" can make some of us feel as if we are failures if we don't have it or don't have enough. That word brings so much anxiety to so many of us.

Having an education is important. It is definitely a plus to be educated, and it is one of the best options we have to live meaningful lives. Education was created not to divide us but *to bring about more perspectives, open up more opinions, and help us communicate and understand each other better.* It was created so that we might become better influencers of each other. (Remember, if we are not influencing positively, we are not living.)

No newborn has an education, yet each infant is born with unique gifts. Such gifts do not require the child to receive an education for it to manifest itself. Babies and children simply need "a good and loving home education," light, truth, patience, and perseverance for their gifts to show themselves. So…we are talking about the fruit of the spirit again! They are the foundation of a fulfilled life.

If a baby is born and grows up with the right amount of positive influences in the ever-so-important formative years of early childhood, and has no privilege of a formal education, his gifts will grow, manifest, and change the world. The gifts will be so nourished, and become so powerful, that they will seek out other ways of growing and branching out, influencing and spreading. Perfect examples of this truth are those children who grow up in poverty or in times of hardship or war but are showered with love, protection, discipline, hope, and wisdom by their parents or other human influencers, and end up being the most influential people in the world—even without the privilege of a formal education. There are countless examples of poorly educated but incredibly successful people, including Mark Twain, author; Albert Einstein, physicist; Steve Jobs, Apple cofounder; John Glenn, astronaut; Abraham Lincoln, US president; Aretha Franklin, entertainer; and Maya Angelou, poet, novelist, actress.

On the other hand, there are those who grow up in wealthy, highly educated families, and who also are highly educated—not just due to their schooling but from people surrounding them who are excellent educational influencers—but who just waste their gifts and do not become positive influences on anyone because they lacked wisdom, love, discipline, self-control, and hope from their parents or responsible parties as they grew up.

The gifts we are born with need the fruit of the spirit to manifest and bloom into their greatest, most meaningful potential. Our gifts need to be watered! They need light and nourishment just like the flowers described earlier.

You can receive the highest, "best" education in the world, but if you have no love, self-control, and kindness in your heart, an education is worthless. So by now I hope you realize that by *education*, I am referring to *formal education*—through school, college, and graduate school—as well as gaining wisdom, direction, hope, and discipline from our parents, responsible parties, caretakers, mentors, and other human influencers as we grow up.

Too often we place all the responsibility of our children's education on teachers and professors, expecting them to impart goodness and wisdom in our kids and forgetting (or neglecting) the strongest education that comes from parents imparting the fruit of the spirit onto them from babyhood and beyond.

Work That Is Magnificent

So if I am supposed to be concentrating on faith and works in this chapter…then why am I talking about people who are positive influencers through using their gifts and the fruit of the spirit? Because we all have to realize where our area of "work" is coming from and what we need to do to grow this "work" into magnificence so that we can continue influencing!

For in this book, work does not necessarily mean a job that we work at each day. Work here means our life-given purposes. It is the magnificent manifestation of the gifts we received at birth as we use them to influence ourselves and others positively. When we do so, it contributes to keeping our two lifelines—our physical and spiritual lines—steady and in forward motion.

Being an influencer fulfills our life purpose and brings us peace, just as we influence others to pursue peace also. Remember, the three steps to pursuing peace, or permanent happiness, are a continuum. One leads to the other, which leads to the other. Our lives fall into meaningful places if we are working on all three simultaneously: (a) consciously changing our characters (living by the fruit of the spirit); (b) nourishing our spiritual and physical lifelines; and (c) using our gifts to positively influence ourselves and others.

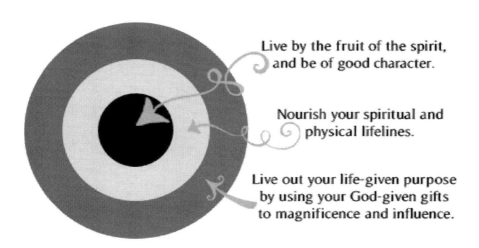

Live by the fruit of the spirit, and be of good character.

Nourish your spiritual and physical lifelines.

Live out your life-given purpose by using your God-given gifts to magnificence and influence.

If you are not influencing others by using the gifts the Creator gave you, your spiritual line will go through many twists and bumps; in many cases, it will come to a standstill and stop moving altogether! *If your lines come to a complete stop and are neither twisting nor in forward motion, you are in trouble and need intervention to get you out of this standstill and moving.* Your own powerful spirit, determination, and courage may be enough to get you out of this standstill, but in many cases you may need intervention from a professional—a therapist, coach, psychologist, or spiritual leader— to get you moving again.

Be aware that twisting and bumpy lines are better than lines that are not moving at all, as these are a sign of a complete loss of hope, despair, and failure. We must do all we can to avoid reaching such a place, but if we arrive there, we must strive to get out quickly by nourishing our physical and spiritual lines continuously and pursuing permanent happiness continually, regardless of circumstance.

Identifying Your Special Gifts

So now we have laid the foundation for why we are given gifts: to be influencers. We understand that we are given gifts that we are born with that are activated with our first cries…but how do we identify what our gifts are?

Your gifts are positive tools or instruments that

- enable you to form routines that make you eagerly look forward to the next day,

- you put into practice and action,

- influence others positively, transforming them and elevating their lives for good, while transforming and elevating you as well.

The universe is set up in a way where we are all wired *to* influence and to *be* influenced; that is why we all have different gifts. There is to be a give-and-take, just as with relationships. *We are here to pour our gifts into each other,* although we can only do this if our environments help us identify our gifts and develop them. If we use our gifts, we can *elevate, influence,* and *transform* children as well as other adults, while at the same time elevating and transforming ourselves.

This is the difference between a person who lives a life of fulfillment…and a person who does not.

Lifting Up

Unfortunately, not every child born into this world has the privilege of having their parents around. Too, not every parent can assume a positive role in their children's lives, for they may not be fit spiritually or physically to assume such a role. Yet we all must have someone to believe in us!

Even if we are parents who are around and there for our children, sometimes we just need to step aside and have an able mentor or coach pour hope, life, inspiration, and love into our children. This does not signify we are not able parents; it just means that at different stages of life, others may be more effective than we would be in lifting up our kids. That is the truth, and that is reality. The fortunate part here is that it gives the rest of us adults the responsibility of being that good role model, influencer, mentor, and advisor for those children or young adults who may be put in our lives somehow and who otherwise would have little or no hope. We are all around other people's children at several points in our lives, and we all have that universe-given responsibility to help the world's children notice their gifts and use them for good.

Once we grow up and turn eighteen, it becomes our turn to be mentors, role models, encouragers, influencers, and advisors. The sooner we all realize this is what the universe and our Creator placed us here for, the sooner we all will get on the path to permanent happiness and a state of inner peace.

Steps to Adulthood

If you have been, and are being, nurtured by an adult and going to school to get an education where you are also being taught and transformed by teachers and other adults, chances are you are beginning to pick up on what your gifts, and your passion, will be as you move into adulthood. If you are a bit unsure, take notice of those acts that make you eagerly want to get up the next morning so that you can influence someone. Those are your *gifts*.

What should you be doing once you have identified some of them? Focus in and improve that skill or skills; research your field of interest, and look for experts in that field to guide you as well. Brainstorm all the possible ways for you to develop your skill to its highest potential: your talent is what is getting you up in the morning. *Seek, ask, find, and knock on doors to get that skill to the point where you can use it to significantly elevate others and yourself.*

This is exactly what I did: From childhood on, I noticed I had gifts of persistence, determination, and organization. Too, I had a somewhat dominant personality. So I used my talents to my advantage and others' advantage by choosing to own my own business and be a leader. Over time, I discovered even more gifts inside of me!

I knew I enjoyed being a pediatrician and taking care of kids, but as time went on, my dominant, determined personality led me into a more managerial, administrative, and supervisory role in my practice. I've discovered this makes me even more fulfilled and gets me up every morning with even more joy and enthusiasm. I noticed that if I was given a task or dreamed up a goal, I could focus in on it, seek out the necessary help, and bring the goal or task to a positive completion. *I had the power in me to achieve my goals.* It helped so much that I had great influencers for my parents: they believed in me, were fully present and engaged in my life, and prayed for me.

Young, soon-to-be-adults: What are your personality traits? Are you the dominant type, a nurturing type, the creative type, or a service-oriented type? Have you noticed your gifts and your main personality type? Have you selected mentors, role models, and influencers who can help you bring the best out of yourself?

But that is only half of the work we must do in our lives… Here comes the harder part: You must stay the course you've identified for yourself to its fulfillment, continuing to manifest your talents and believe in yourself. No true fulfillment comes without curiosity, hard work, perseverance, suffering, self-control, humility, and respect for authority. Those latter three are huge in importance. HUGE, HUGE, HUGE, my friends.

Three Traits Lead You to Your Highest Potential

Self-control, humility, and respect for authority are the three traits that will get you to your fullest and highest potential. Why? In a nutshell, there are many great influencers all around us, but many of us miss out on this influence as we carry a pitiful and unnecessary air of arrogance, defensiveness, and self-righteousness around with us.

Let go and let in. Allow those wonderful and talented influencers out there to get through to you!

Disrespect of authority is the surest path to failure. If you want to fail, just do one thing and do it continuously: belittle or disregard those in authority. If you disrespect your parents, caregivers, teachers, college professors, bosses, police officers, the law, sales clerks, and the president, it is the worst thing for you! We all must be humble and respect others, regardless of their status, position, or age, or whether they have wronged us or not.

That last one might be very hard for us. You might ask me, *Why should I respect someone who has wronged me or wronged others who look like and belong to the same group as me?* Well, because you are you, and they are them. You are an individual, flanked by your physical and spiritual lines, and no one is with you in between those lines. You, and you alone, are responsible for *you*. You are not responsible for them. Focus on yourself, do the right thing, stay in forward motion in the middle of your lines…and you will surely succeed!

Give those other people—even those who have wronged you—time and space to figure themselves out. Focus on what is magical about you being you, and act with self-control and respect regardless of others' behavior toward you. If you do, you will be an influencer and eventually transform them. You just have to be patient.

Some of the biggest challenges in our world come from our youth, young adults, and even some adults continuously disrespecting authority—and then their lives start failing and spiraling out of control. We are losing so many children's lives because of this—and adults, we are to blame! Yes, we are. We are not teaching our children the importance of self-control, humility, and respect for authority. It is not always necessary or wise to react in some circumstances; in some situations, gentleness and humility are just the "way to be."

I am grateful that I was born into a home where I was taught from a young age, "You must respect your elders, your teachers, and the law." My parents taught me not to talk back to people of authority. They told me to be quiet, to keep my lips zipped up, to hush up, and to obey my elders and everyone in authority, regardless of their age, status, or what I thought of them.

If you respect those in authority, it will transform your life and bring you success in every area of your life. Now, this does not mean you must be a softy or not have a voice of your own. I am trying to get across that we must be gentle, humble, confident, and fearless advocates for ourselves—*but not through disrespect of authority, arrogance, or controlling behavior.* You are not letting go of your own power by respecting authority. You actually are claiming your power and owning it as you respect everyone who comes along. Exhibiting calm and controlled behavior shows you are a self-reconciled person, and that is a great trait to have.

We all have a choice, and it's an easy one: **Disrespect authority and fail in life. Or respect authority and succeed in life.** It's up to each one of us to get on to the right and true path.

Power over Your Future

Forgetting your past hurts is also so important to manage and own. From generation to generation to generation, people have wronged other people...*but what good does it do to hold on to past grievances?* **We have absolutely no power over the past, whereas we have great power over the future.**

The past has only one purpose: to teach us lessons and wisdom that we can use for making our futures better.

Holding on to, and focusing on, past hurts is another sure path to failure. If all you are doing is reliving the past and reminding yourself of all the hurts done to you, your loved ones, or your community, you are slowly destroying yourself. Holding on to the pain of the past holds you in tight bondage and separates your soul and spirit from divine, heavenly connection. You are no use to yourself or to others if you are in such bondage!

The past is already gone; that time is no longer here. It has slipped away. However, if we can get a grip on the future and make it better, we can slowly get on the path of permanent happiness—that state of peace we all crave. It's up to each one of us to get on this right and true path. You can do so by *rechanneling all that energy you are expending on reliving the past into making the future better.*

Your heart, soul, body, mind, and spirit will thank you for letting go of the past, because they will now be able to get through to you and guide you toward living the awesome, meaningful life that was meant for you.

Why Give Up?

The phrase "Nothing good comes easy" is very true. We are all aware that hard work, perseverance, and persistence pay off, so why do we quit so easily? Why do we give up so quickly and spend our entire lives looking for greener or easier pastures?

I am not suggesting that greener pastures do not exist. Of course they do, but we will come across them only if we have done our best, worked with all the tools and gifts we have, obeyed the rules, and respected the authority figures around us.

It is puzzling to me how some employees spend their entire time on the job disrespecting their bosses or supervisors and having chips on their shoulders. They come in to work late, break the rules, fail to meet deadlines, and have constantly negative and defensive attitudes. Then they go on to quit their jobs…and they blame their bosses or coworkers for it not working out!

I tell you, when people like that go about seeking a "better" job…that better job will never come! The problem is not the boss. It is not the coworkers. It is them, their traits, their behaviors, and their attitudes.

How do you go about succeeding at a job? Persevere, don't quit, work hard, and do your best in your current job. Stand tall, put a smile on your face, and be grateful that you have a job. Count your blessings, and if you have a negative attitude, replace it with humility and positivity. Listen to your boss, follow the rules, and look for ways to improve your skills on the job. Show up fifteen minutes early—or even earlier—to get a jump on the workday. Stop counting up and stressing about every second or minute you have had to work overtime. Be respectful and nonjudgmental of others. Spread love and wisdom among your colleagues, and exhibit a gentle confidence…and success will be yours! Trust me on this. However, first do it *for your own inner peace, not for your boss.* However, the reality is, with time your boss and other colleagues will notice, and you will be acknowledged and rewarded.

Imperfect jobs are paths to perfect jobs. How can you come to know what is perfect for you if you have not yet poured your heart, your gifts, and your positive instruments into your line of work and job and stayed the course to see what manifests from it? If you don't do this, you will repeat the same mistakes at your next job. And the next. Allow the influencer or influencers in your job to influence you for good to prepare you for the next level in your life. Stay the course.

One Rung at a Time

What is a ladder for? Why does it have rungs? The answer is pretty obvious: we use ladders to get to a higher place, such as a ceiling, a roof, or another kind of higher level to seek out something. And how do we get there? One step at a time.

Do you step on one rung, then give up and turn back down and give up on that leaky roof, or that piece of jewelry, or that other important document you are looking for in the top of your cabinet or attic? No, you don't. You step up the ladder one rung at a time until you get to your destination, fix the leaky roof, or find what you are looking for.

Friends, please continue on those rungs one step at a time and head on up to that roof, that ceiling, that higher place. Seek out, then look into, that cabinet or higher place to find what you are looking for. You may not end up fixing or finding the item you are looking for, but you will come down knowing you took it one step at a time and you moved up, and you put some effort into trying to reach your goal. That's how you should be on the job: Be persistent, be courageous, do it one step at a time, and stay the course. You will find what you need for a fulfilling work life if you take one step at a time to reach that higher, sought-after place.

Some things in life are guaranteed, and that is the case here: if you work hard, respect authority, seek able mentors, and stay the course, you will reap great success.

When Adversity Empowers

The word *adversity* usually has negative connotations, but did you ever realize that adversity can transform a lot of people for the good? Have you ever noticed that many successful, fulfilled people have had periods of adversity where they thought their lives were spiraling out of control and had lost hope, but then they made important changes and key shifts…and their lives started to evolve and become a thousand times better?

God-given power lies within us and can enable us to elevate ourselves out of failures. So we can all use adversity to our own advantage.

Adversity can be empowering! It stirs up restlessness and curiosity in us and makes us seek answers and solutions to our problems with passion and vengeance. As adversity does not feel good, it is natural for us to want to get out of it. It is a knock on the door of our souls, urging us that it is time for change, time for growth, and time to do greater and better things. Adversity is *not* a knock urging you to start worrying, live in fear and anxiety, and panic about what may happen if you take action. It is a knock urging you to utilize the power you have to hurdle past, and grow beyond, the specific adversity. You just must tap into the God-given power inside you, believe in the strength of your power, and use it to overcome and depart from that adversity.

Too many stay in adverse life situations for way too long, finding excuse after excuse for staying until the situation eventually cripples them. But if we stay in negative situations, they suppress our gifts, our influences, and our processes of permanent happiness/peace.

So do not allow hopelessness, worry, and fear to pin you down so that you stay in adverse situations for longer than needed. Allow your God-given power to take over and lift you out of a place of despair. Adversity is in your life to teach you a lesson. Grab that lesson, run with it, and use it to your magnificence. Do not look back!

I have had my own share of adversity in my life, lasting for a period of seven years. I'll summarize. During the time I was dealing with a new business, a newborn, and a sister who died of cancer, my marriage blew up and became such a hostile divorce that our home was repossessed not because of our inability to pay, but because both parties were unwilling to cooperate with each other. So those were really tough years, but guess what? I was tougher. I held on to my God-given power, and it gave me the toughness, resilience, and hope to push through.

I had no choice but to *not* give up and to keep fighting so I could use my presence on this earth and my God-given gifts to their full magnificence. You see, I was fully aware I still had work to do on this earth to become a great influencer, so I pushed through by trying as hard as I could to stay in the middle of my spiritual and physical lines, even though they were rapidly bending and very much out of control. But I stayed the course, using all the power within me to get my lines back to steady and flowing again in forward motion.

As I mentioned earlier in my life story, I soon met a wonderful man who brought me hope and was the perfect breath of fresh air I needed! He made me laugh like I had never laughed before, and we traveled the world together. He was the angel God sent to me to help me back on my feet. He was my great influencer and encourager.

I pushed through, I did not give up, and I came out of this period of great adversity a better, stronger person. Yes, life is certain to continue to bring uncertainties and issues my way; it's unavoidable. However, I am fully aware that responding with fear, fragility, and hopelessness is *optional*. And I do not choose this option.

Use adversity to your advantage too. It is a path to *appreciation*. You cannot fully appreciate the manifestation of your own God-given gifts without experiencing adversity.

So adversity is humbling, it is empowering, and it is a necessary tool for strength and success. Once again, do not let adverse times and events in your life cripple you. Push through, forgive, love, heal, let go…and let more, and better, in.

Poison to the Soul

WORRY is poison to the soul. It is the exact opposite of faith and gentle confidence. Living in this state will slowly consume you and leave your spiritual and physical lives sick, almost to the point of death.

Worry is why so many of us suffer from insomnia, get addicted to sleeping pills and other drugs or substances, and suffer from a host of medical, mental, and psychological issues.

However, my friends, nobody is born a worrier. And worry does not solve any problems. It just makes the problem worse tenfold.

If you are worrying about something to a level where it has caused you physical and spiritual illness, you are missing out on the power given to you by our Creator! You have completely abandoned the power that lies within you—and that is a waste.

Why worry chronically about something that *you* have the power to change? All that time and energy you spent worrying, tossing and turning in bed, could have transformed your life, one step at a time, one rung at a time. *Anything that is keeping you up at night needs immediate attention and action.*

You must make changes and shifts immediately! Enough with procrastination and waiting for faith to pull you through this sad state. Faith is good, but without using your God-given power to act, make changes, and walk away from, say, that toxic relationship, or work toward solving that problem or achieving that dream, your faith is worthless. **You must work and act...and then have faith to "seal the deal"!**

Be a Doer, Not a Worrier

The next time you stay up at night all worried and unable to sleep, try this exercise before popping another pill: Get out a pen and paper and draw a ladder with rungs. Then, step by step on each rung, write down your plan for solving this issue that is keeping you up at night. Be completely honest with yourself and write down only specific, tangible, and practical action steps that you can take. Honesty is key here. If you can only come up with one or two steps in the middle of the night, that is still perfectly fine. You would have at least started the process. As more solutions pop into your mind during the following days, add more steps.

Also specify exactly what you are feeling and thinking at the moment. Do not deny your true thoughts and beliefs. Also, do not start by writing on the first step, "I am praying and believing in God that this will happen." That is a perfect and strong prayer, of course, but you must place that prayer and affirmation *at the very top step,* once you are done with writing all your practical action steps first. That faith prayer will then seal the deal for all your action steps.

So let's say you need to find a job. For the lowest, very first rung, write down something like, "I will start to attend more networking events." Rung two could be something like, "I will start to read more about that line of work." Then, "I will look for a mentor to clarify some questions I have." "I will work on improving my interviewing skills." "I may have to work without pay for a while to get my skills noticed." "I will accept a less-than-desirable position until I land my dream job."

Create as many steps or rungs as you think you will need on your ladder. Then at the top step and final rung, put down your faith prayer. Read and affirm all the steps and the faith prayer at the top at bedtime and at other times during the day if you wish. In no time, your life will be transformed! Trust me: it works.

How about doing this as your routine instead of popping off some sleeping pill instead?! Your body, soul, spirit, and mind will thank you for it.

Worriers tend not to be doers. If you are concerned about a life situation, or you have a desire, or you want to see key changes in your life, or long for a passion, you have two choices. *You worry*, or *you do.*

Worriers have no faith, and they are always fearful. Doers are fearless, and they have a lot of faith.

Realize this too: doing and working toward your goals and passion may sometimes keep you up at night, *but in a good way.* It keeps you up because your mind is full of ideas, strategies, and vivid pictures that cannot wait to burst out and influence others. Even if you occasionally experience the less-than-required number of sleep hours as a result, you will wake up energized because your soul is being nourished.

Seal the Deal with Faith

Each one of us was created to be a great influencer. So believe in your greatness. Open the doors and windows around you, and ask worry, fear, and doubt to exit from your life and never come back. If you do not believe in yourself and have faith in yourself, no one else will believe in you or have faith in you.

Now, I'd like to define *faith* as follows: faith is that firm belief, that confidence, that significant hope, that even though we have not yet seen the results of our works, our works will eventually manifest for good if we stay the course, play our parts, and keep on dreaming and visualizing the results.

Our *works* are what make us potentially great and fulfilled influencers, while our *faith* allows this influencer status we have to manifest in this world.

It Is Never Too Late to Discover Your Gifts!

As for discovering one of my own "works"…I started to write this book in 2015, and its contents inspire me to this day. As described earlier, I often had to stop in the middle of other tasks to write down ideas and new thoughts for this book. I also stayed up late at night, woke up early, and stayed in on some evenings to write because I was not able to control the *automatic* urge in me to keep on writing! The creation was a spiritual experience for me—and so fulfilling.

I know my book is a gift from a higher source because as I write, and go back to review some of the content, I am intrigued by what I have written—and sometimes even wonder if I truly was the one who came up with these ideas! The process was so automatic for me that it largely felt like an out-of-body experience. I have the confidence and assurance in my deepest soul that the writing of it was a higher calling from above and that my book will eventually reach a phenomenal number of people all around the world and inspire them to transform their lives. Inner peace and joy comes from knowing that I will get to share this wisdom with the world. I am visualizing the end result…and I see *great influencing as a result of my fellow humans reading this book.*

Now, while writing was a positive instrument bestowed on me by God, I only became fully aware of this gift *at forty-five years of age!* I did feel small urges in my past trying to tell me to write, 'tis true, but I had too much going on, and I just could not focus in at those times. So let my story tell you...*it is never too late.* As I noted earlier, the gifts are in us from birth, waiting for an opportune time to be explored, nourished, and manifested for good. I am nourishing one of my gifts now, and already it is completely transforming my life.

Is your gift, or several of your gifts, still lying dormant in you? If so, are you fully aware of what is preventing them from manifesting? It may be time to connect with your spirit and find out what that gift is, and exactly what is preventing its manifestation.

Have you written down your action steps on the rungs of the ladder as just described? Are you stepping out and doing these action steps? Are you actually believing the manifestation of your gifts will be great? Are you visualizing the manifestation in great detail? And are you surrounding yourself with up to three able coaches or mentors? (Or are you still listening to the noise and buzzing voices of the opinions of ten to twenty friends/family or acquaintances?) Who are you influencing with your gifts, your works, and your faith?

My Personal Works and Faith (as of This Writing)

As I started the new year (2017), I wrote down my hopes and affirmations for my life for this year and beyond, and I continuously read them again and again. I visualize every fine detail of what I hope for, and I work toward my hopes and believe they will manifest. My current ones are my first book reaching many lives, and discovering the wonderful man who will become a part of my life as we grow and share life together.

As I work on my life purpose, transform and elevate myself, and find fulfillment and inner peace, I am preparing for that special, unique man whom I believe I will be meeting soon. I believe that within me I have been preparing for this man, as I have slowly transformed myself spiritually. I finally feel ready to receive him into my life.

What are your examples of works and faith? What are you currently working on or dreaming and hoping for? Again, have your positive instruments been lying dormant in you?

My hope is for this chapter to help you notice those gifts, and for you to start working diligently on their full manifestation and eventual influence, and to hold on to faith and the assurance that *you can get it done!*

Chapter 6

Our Spiritual Lives

If you keep chasing after life and its chaos, craziness, and routines, and do not carve out time to quietly connect with your spirit, you will fail at living a meaningful life.

Is your life always go-go-go, completely consumed with the hustle and bustle of living? Do you have to work through and manage numerous deadlines, work tasks, traffic, long commutes, and the impatience and road rage of others? Is your household (or you) about to explode as you strive to get your kids to activities, make their meals, and correct their poor food choices and lack of portion control? Is your body suffering from little to no physical activity, a lack of sleep, the use of sleeping pills, substance abuse, alcohol intoxication, and/or caffeine overconsumption? Is your self-esteem poor or very low? Is your mind always running at about one hundred miles an hour all through the day as you think about all you have to do, do, do?

Some of us have days like this day in and day out. Well, if you are living your life like this, you are not living; you are just existing. You will just keep going and going on your treadmill until your soul gets weakened to the point of non-recovery, and you will completely stop existing due to a chronically irreversible illness or from death. You see, you cannot continue at such a fast, unchecked pace without completely burning out or gradually fading away.

Your spirit is your nucleus; it is what centers and grounds you. And so you must actively nurture it. Most of us have routines for other aspects of our lives, but we fail to include time dedicated to our spiritual well-being…*the most important aspect of our existence!* And if it takes a backseat, as it often does, our lives seemingly work for a while, then suddenly fall apart. Then it takes us a lot of effort, intervention, and yes, medical attention to get our lives back on track. Some of us, unfortunately, never get our spiritual health back, and our lives fail and fall apart completely.

Yet if we nurture and strengthen our spirits and maintain life-spirit connections, those connections keep us strong and grounded and prepare us for the difficult times that will surely come.

The Importance of Spirit

Your spirit has a lot to say to you, for there is a direct line of connection between your spirit and the heavenly Father. But only in times of perfect solitude and stillness can we be fully receptive and able to hear from God. We need alone time, connecting with our spirits and hearing how we should be manifesting our God-given gifts to greatness. We must listen to know who we are meant to really be, to find out God's plans for our lives, to discern what we should get rid of and who we should distance ourselves from, to understand the key shifts in our lives that need to be made, and to visualize the positive people waiting to enter our lives and influence us for good.

We cannot fully connect with the spiritual realm if we do not carve out alone time to fully rest our spirits and hear all these messages. It is a pleasure to spend time with friends and loved ones, but it is equally important to spend time alone, connecting with our own essences and recharging our souls and our heart issues by connecting our spirits directly with our Creator and heavenly Father. *If we do not recharge and refuel our spirits daily, we will not do well with relationships and with life in general.* We must guard, recharge, and protect our hearts on a daily basis, for out of the heart comes the wellspring of life.

Some of us start to "get" the importance of spirituality in middle age or old age after life's unforeseen circumstances have struck us over and over. And unfortunately, a lot of us never, ever will appreciate the importance of the spiritual connection.

Truly, though, the best time to understand and honor the spiritual connection is in the teenage or youth years so we can fully live out lives of peace, joy, and purpose. The rewards are so much greater if we appreciate the spiritual connection then.

Time for Time-Out

When was the last time you took time out to listen? Do you have enough time and stillness in your day to notice all the signs being sent to you from a higher place? If you quiet your soul and spirit, you will clearly hear and visualize all the positive messages being sent to you from our Creator and from your angels.

Your life-spirit connection is so important…but *how many of us have **developed a routine** for our spiritual well-being?* I'm suggesting a planned, daily quiet and still time with our eyes closed and disconnecting from all the noise in our heads and the noise from without. A time when we are, perhaps, meditating and listening to uplifting, empowering, gentle music; taking a walk in nature with no time constraints; having a dedicated and planned time for prayer; and worshipping in a holy place—a church, temple, or mosque, for example.

If you are too restless to completely disconnect and quiet your mind during your alone time, then here are some suggestions as to how you can get in touch with your spiritual side:

- Take up journaling.

- Create a vision board.

- Read the Bible or another holy book.

- Read an inspirational or spiritual book or a collection of affirmations by others (or personal ones that you have compiled for yourself).

- Listen to "good music" (not the heavy, intense music that gets your heart pounding and has negative and derogatory musical lyrics that seep into your soul and put your soul in turmoil, but gentle, uplifting music to calm the mind and

117

forge a spiritual connection).

I've discovered some great gospel songs, as well as others songs that are soft pop with positive lyrics, to listen to during my alone time. A few of my personal favorites are "Speak to My Heart" and "Stand," by Donnie McClurkin; "Oceans," by Hillsong United; "What a Beautiful Name," by Hillsong Worship; "Death Was Arrested," by North Point Music; "How He Loves Us," by David Crowder; and "Remedy" and "When We Were Young," by Adele. These songs have empowered me and given me hope. They always bring a smile to my face and peace to my soul. If you find you don't like inspirational gospel, perhaps listen to some calming classical music or smooth jazz right before you light a white candle, (safety first— please use appropriate caution with candles) and visualize light and peace in your surroundings. There are many ways to quiet your soul so you can hear its voice.

Daily Rest for the Soul

You will never connect to your deepest soul during all the chaos and distractions of life. You will never be able to have clear focus and direction in your life if you don't take time out daily to rest your soul and really connect your ongoing life with your spirit. **Doing so is a life necessity. It's not a choice but a "must-do" in order to really experience life in its richness.** The nourishment and sustenance of our spiritual lives or lifelines is essential for permanent happiness/peace. If you keep chasing after life and its chaos, craziness, and routines and do not carve out time to quietly connect with your spirit, you will fail at living a meaningful life. This is not a "maybe it will happen"; it is a "surely it will happen!" It is just a matter of time before it does.

When was the last time you really noticed your breath, your inhalations and exhalations, how you fill your lungs with oxygen and then release it? When was the last time you stepped outside and thanked God for that cold or warm air that touched your face and the breath of fresh air you just inhaled? Have you expressed gratitude for the elegant trees, the bright flowers, and the chirping of the birds? When did you last notice the amazingly beautiful sunrise and sunset outside your window? The beauty of a full moon? How about the innocent giggling of toddlers at a park?

So much of life's beauty we miss every day because we are so consumed with life's heavy distractions. Let go of the heaviness of life, and embrace the lightness of life. The lightness of life feels so much better, and it cleanses and refreshes our souls.

For some of us, noticing the simple moments and lightness in life all around us just never happens, or it used to happen a long time ago, when we were much younger and innocent, carefree children. We must start to notice all this loveliness all around us again. It is there for a reason: to help us detach from life's never-ending burdens.

The Best Antiaging Medicine Ever!

Now, let's consider our spiritual health from another perspective: did you know the best antiaging medicine is spiritual awareness, stillness of mind, and appreciation of self?

No? How about this, then: isn't it so easy to tell a person whose life is chaotic by how much they have aged?

There is no plastic surgery solution that will hide the chaos your life is in. *Inner peace will make you radiate and glow like the sun!* It will take years off your real age and make others wonder if there is a "secret" to your eternally youthful appearance.

Spiritual awareness and health freshens your skin, eliminates your wrinkles, reduces inflammation in your body, strengthens your immune system, and rewires and strengthens your brain. Most importantly, it helps you flash that smile and gives you a great posture and gentle confidence and assurance that everything will be okay, regardless of all of life's circumstances. You can stand tall, and your very presence, without you even saying a word, just uplifts those around you. What an awesome effect!

Wouldn't we all love to have the effect of what the state of permanent happiness—PEACE—does to us?!

Clean and purify your insides by being more spiritually connected, and your outside will become clean too. Spiritual health is directly related to physical health. There are so many illnesses and ailments that originate from the lack of a life-spirit connection, including inflammatory bowel disease, digestive problems, cancers, heart disease, weight issues, sleep issues, addictive behaviors, psychological and self-esteem disorders, and so many others.

The Power of Positive People

Your relationships are a vital part of your spiritual health. So please, please, please choose the company you keep carefully, and only surround yourself with people who practice and believe in positive thinking.

Your goal is to find people who are actively and steadily in the middle of their physical and spiritual lines. They are living by the fruit of the spirit and are in the process of pursuing peace. Such individuals are genuine, authentic, stable, loyal, dependable, and forward moving. They are great influencers and great motivators, whether this be in small or big ways.

Never underestimate the power of others on you. Life is about influencing and being influenced. Allow other great influencers to strengthen your spiritual lifeline.

How can you find these kinds of people, practically speaking? Find like-minded people

- at your place of worship,
- at a book club,
- at your workplace,
- online,
- through shared and similar interests or hobbies.

And when you do…encourage one another without ceasing!

Peaceful Spaces

Do you live and work in a cluttered, unclean space? What does your home look like? Your office space? How about your car or your bedroom? Are there piles of rubbish and stuff everywhere in your home and in your car?

We cannot have spiritual awareness, connection, and stillness in spaces that look like disorganized, cluttered messes. It is impossible. The spaces and surroundings around us should evoke calmness and peace.

The level of disorganization in your surroundings directly reflects the chaos going on in your mind, and it will translate into chaos in every aspect of your life. *We must clean out our environments so we can clean out our souls and spirits.*

If you walk into a bedroom with clean white sheets, a newly vacuumed carpet, a lamp shining in one corner, the windows open letting in the sunshine and fresh air, and everything put away in its place, you will immediately feel a calming of the spirit. The same applies to your office environment and car too.

A dirty, cluttered car reveals the state of your soul. (No wonder there is so much road rage. I wonder if a study could be done to see if there is a direct relationship between unclean, messy cars and road rage. It would not surprise me if there is.) We must start to routinely de-clutter and clean all our living spaces, and we must teach our children to do the same. It will positively change their lives too in every way.

Managing the Crossroads

With every crossroads I have come to, connecting in some way with my spiritual essence has helped me gain clarity as to the next action to take.

Around the time of my divorce, I found journaling helped me keep my thoughts organized. I also journaled a lot around the opening of my practice, and I actually still do now surrounding my medical practice operations. Journaling helps me really visualize what my mind is thinking, and I am better able to come to terms with that and take the appropriate action(s).

After the crossroads of my father's passing, I would just sit in stillness in the quiet of my bedroom and try to connect with his spirit, sometimes with lit candles, and often with inspirational music playing. I felt him close to me every time I did this, and it brought peace to my spirit.

During other times of crisis, I enjoyed arriving early to church. I would just sit there quietly, taking in the environment, watching, observing, and saying hello to people as they walked by me and found seats. It gave me a sense of peace knowing we were all gathering for a common purpose.

There are signs all around us, messages waiting to be imparted in our souls, if only we will quiet our minds and connect with our spirits. Here's one example.

On January 3, 2016, my daughters and I arrived early at our church, and as we sat in our car waiting, (my older daughter had driven us there), I decided that this moment was an opportune time to inform them about this book I'd been writing. I explained in detail and told them it was about living by the fruit of the spirit, how we had to have joy, love, and self-control in our hearts in order to have peace or permanent happiness. I also discussed the importance of our spiritual and physical lines. Well, would you believe that in the service that day, the pastor's sermon turned out to be about everything I had just shared with my daughters in the car?! The screens and monitors all popped up with Galatians 5:22, *The fruit of the spirit!* I had goose bumps all through that service, and the knowledge filled my eyes with tears.

This sequence of events was sending me a message from above assuring me I had a good concept to share in my book. Those two moments (with my daughters and in church after with the pastor) were a connection with my spirit and God's validation on my work that I was getting ready to share with the world.

Validating Moments

I believe there are many moments in all our lives that help validate what we are doing and who we are. But if we are too busy running around, chasing deadlines, arriving and showing up late because of poor time management, living chaotic lives, numbing our pain with drugs and alcohol, and filling our hearts and minds with worry or other dark thoughts like chronic envy and the like, we will never hear or see these messages and signs. *Those signs are there to direct our paths. They are signs of divine guidance.*

When was the last time you stilled your spirit enough to receive a message or sign that would direct the course of your life? If the answer is, "Never," or "I can't remember," or "It has been a while," it is time to pay attention to your spiritual life and how you are nourishing it. *It is time to start scheduling a daily sacred spiritual time.*

Having quiet, sacred times during the day, every day, and guarding our hearts from negative thoughts enables us to have dreams that are actually notices and messages from God. I have had a number of these dreams that have come true, such as the dream I shared of my dad's passing.

Weaknesses for Good

We must also learn to capitalize on our weaknesses—on our traits that are not our strengths—and make them work for good. This means we must make peace with aspects of ourselves and of our lives of which we may not be completely proud.

Our weaknesses are actually here and present to help us excel and do better in other areas of life. So the weaknesses we have may be there to create spaces in our lives for our strengths to magnify themselves. But we can only realize this if we still our spirits enough and look for the good in the weaknesses.

For example, as I mentioned before, I am not a fan of driving. I can drive, but it gives me restless, panicky feelings, so I now hire services like Uber to take me where I need to go. The point I'm making is this: I have learned to utilize my time sitting in the back of these rides *to my own good and to improve my spiritual awareness!* What an opportunity it has turned out to be! I no longer have to deal with the traffic, chaos, rising tempers, and road rage going on around me. Instead, I sit in a comfortable car, sip my tea or coffee, and use the time to return emails and refine my to-do list and goals for the day and week. Sometimes I just enjoy some quiet time listening to my own music with my earbuds on, or I stare out the window appreciating the beauty of nature and my surroundings. I also enjoy having conversations with the driver of the car, as I get to learn about and understand some other life perspectives. I arrive at my destinations now with a calm spirit ready to start my day or engage in whatever my destination holds for me.

Also, since I started writing this book, I have been able to gather content while sitting in the peacefulness of the car, just typing away on my iPad. My "driving" time is now *a time of achieving spiritual awareness for me*—and I have no regrets about not driving anymore! I have learned to use the time completely to my own benefit and the benefit of others, as I always arrive in peace and calm, ready to interact positively with people. So do I consider not driving a weakness anymore? *Absolutely not!*

A few months ago on Facebook, I saw the news of a fellow physician who had passed away. She was about my age, and while she practiced as a physician here in the United States, she had attended the same secondary school as I did in Lagos, Nigeria. As I read all the good wishes and prayers to her and her family, I stumbled on a video of her that had been recorded the previous year while she was still battling cancer. As I listened to what she had lived with, I froze and teared up. It turned out she had battled the same driving phobia I had—but had not found an alternative! From her speech it seemed that this phobia had caused her a lot of grief, sadness, and angst; she struggled through life trying to drive, even though she panicked all throughout the drives. She said she attributed the constant panicking that went on over several years, and its effects on her body and physiologic state, to the cancer she eventually developed. Whether that played a part in her cancer or not, no one can really know. Of course, there were likely other factors, but you get the picture here: *your spiritual state is directly related to your physical state.* So every dollar I spend on being driven around has been an investment in calming my spirit and making sure my physiological state is in balance. Experiencing panic and anxiety constantly increases our heart rate and releases stress hormones that wreak major havoc on our bodies.

To me, nourishing our spirits and bringing calm into our souls is the answer to all our woes. We must do all we can to save our souls and calm our spirits, no matter the cost or price.

So…it is okay to have weaknesses. We all cannot be great at everything.

It's Okay!

It is okay if you…

- do not fit in;
- are not part of the majority;
- can't drive;
- have some disability;
- are not as "privileged" as others are;
- are just starting off, whereas all your friends have achieved a lot already; and/or
- are going through a divorce, whereas all your friends are all seemingly happily married.

It is all okay! Every one of us still has enormous power within us despite our weaknesses. So hold your head up high—and grab the alternative that is better for you! Adjust your lifestyle, make it work—*and watch yourself soar.*

Reject the people who mock you because of your weakness(es). (But do this with love and manners.) You don't need them around you if they are not secure people.

Insecure people always have the goal to magnify others' weaknesses in order to minimize theirs.

Making Weaknesses into Tools

Weaknesses are not signs of failure! *They are tools to help you strengthen another area of your life.* So embrace your weaknesses, and thank God for allowing those weaknesses to help you find and develop your greatness.

But without spiritual awareness and being in a place of peace and confidence, you will continue to look at your weaknesses as failures and miss out on the good they are actually meant to bring into your life.

Every adversity and weakness has an advantage. In every weak or adverse part of your life, there is a light shining somewhere. Still your spirit, and connect with your soul so you can see that light. Others may try to put you down because of the weakness, but as long as you know you are gaining strength from those circumstances, you are well on your way to freedom and greatness.

Can you identify any weak area of your life that has empowered you to increased strength and greatness in another aspect of your life? Write it down today, and be thankful for it.

Remember this: Those who want to magnify other people's weaknesses to pull others down have major, deep-seated self-esteem issues. You are not the problem; they are. I have had friends and significant others laugh about and make fun of the fact that I do not like driving or that I panic while driving or sitting in a fast-moving car. But I also have friends who have been understanding and supportive. Well, guess what? This situation helped me know who my true and real friends are!

Lift your head up high, ignore those who mock you, own your weaknesses, and use them to your magnificence. We cannot put our hope and trust in others. We must trust our Creator instead, who accepts and loves us unconditionally, imperfections and all.

Be Grateful and Rejoice

Another essential part of nourishing our spiritual lives is by *always being grateful for what we currently have.* Gratitude heals, renews, and refreshes the spirit. If we cannot appreciate and embrace all that life has given us to date, we will misuse what is still to come.

So…count your blessings, always. Rejoice and give thanks; there is no better way for a fast and easy path to strengthen your ever-so-vital spiritual lifeline!

Chapter 7

Our Physical Lives

Excuses and denial are major deterrents to achieving weight goals!
Face the problem; fix the problem.

Why do people write or buy book after book after book featuring a different diet for fast and quick weight loss? Because body-image issues, and weight issues, contribute immensely to quality of life.

If you are experiencing physical or psychological problems from being overweight or obese, then you must do something to lose weight and get back on track. The same goes for the other end of the spectrum, anorexia and bulimia—these also lead to the same problems. Weight issues can lead to major self-esteem problems that last a lifetime and are emotionally crippling.

Our physical and spiritual lives flank us as two parallel lines, but they are very tightly connected. The situation is a bit like the chicken-and-the-egg theory: Which one leads to which? Is my spiritual health suffering because my physical health is suffering? Or is my physical health suffering because my spiritual health is suffering? The correct answer to both is *yes*.

If you are unhappy from being overweight or obese, or anorexic or bulimic, experiencing self-esteem problems, and/or major psychological conditions like depression and anxiety, and have chronic medical illnesses, your spiritual life will suffer! If you are not connecting with your spirit regularly, being still and hearing the voice of your soul speak to you and strengthen you from inside, your physical life will suffer too. This could result in overeating and obesity and also in different illnesses and ailments. So it's clear how our two lifelines are ever so important: *If one goes out of balance, the other follows. You cannot pay attention to one, actively nourish it, and then ignore the other one if you want to experience a good quality of life.*

Healthy Physical Sustenance

The following are key aspects to sustaining a healthy physical life. All are equally important for nourishing and maintaining your physical lifeline. While I am not an expert in the field of nutrition and physical activity, I will share what I know works and has helped me maintain my weight at a healthy level.

- **THE TYPES OF FOOD WE EAT**

We must eat a balanced diet daily—with the key word here being *balanced*. Many diets eliminate one food group completely or focus on liquid intake only. I am not condemning or criticizing any of these diets, but our diet must be *balanced* as the following USDA food graphic illustrates.

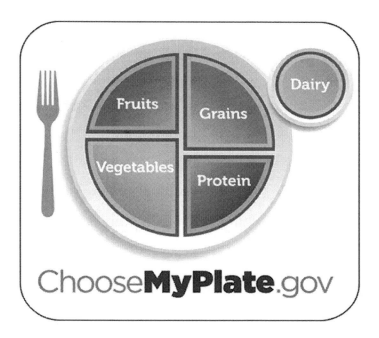

ChooseMyPlate.gov

The largest food groups that we should consume daily are veggies and whole grains. This is followed by fruits and then healthy proteins, such as fish and eggs. And don't forget healthy fats, such as avocados and nuts.

Most of the current diet fads reverse the portion order. As a nation, we are consuming more red meat, chicken, carbs, and refined sugars (soda is included in refined sugars). Well, if our bodies should be taking in certain types of foods but we are not doing so, we are asking for trouble.

Notice there is no *processed food* portion on this diagram. This is because it is imperative that we cut out processed foods as much as possible and prepare and consume foods from their raw, pure, organic state. (*Processed foods* are foods which have been canned, frozen, preserved with high amounts of sodium, and/or enriched with lots of added sugar and/or trans fats. Examples are canned meats, frozen dinners, microwave dinners, and packs of cookies.) It is important that we are familiar with, and knowledgeable about, food labeling and nutritional contents of what we are consuming daily.

The current obesity epidemic is real and only getting worse. So the first thing we must know before we take action is what we should be eating every day: *a healthy balance of the MyPlate different food groups in the proportions suggested.* Please choose more veggies; whole, unrefined grains; fresh fruits; healthy nuts; and much less red meat, bread, cake, soda, and sweets.

- **PORTION CONTROL**

The next most important point in terms of what we eat is that we have all become disconnected and detached from recognizing our satiety levels. *We do not know when we are full anymore, and so we eat through our satisfaction and fullness levels.*

This is somewhat surprising, as our brains are naturally wired to inform us on when we should stop eating. So we actually should know when we are full. Why don't we?

Children are born with the ability to know when they are full and when they need to stop eating. However, many adults have an erroneous perception of how much children should eat and how their kids should look. So they constantly overfeed their children, trying to make them eat more and more in the misguided belief that the kids are not eating enough! Eventually the youngsters become unable to perceive their satiety levels anymore and get used to eating many times more food than what their bodies need. If this happens, the problem often stays with the children into adulthood.

It amazes me in my practice as a pediatrician how many kids with a normal body mass index (BMI) percentile (weight to height ratio) are brought in by their parents demanding that tests be run or medications to be prescribed since their children "look too thin, so they must be sick." Yet their kids are usually just fine, with BMIs between the 25th and 75th percentiles—and that's absolutely normal!

Why is it that obese or overweight kids in the 85th percentile and above seem to never get brought in for consideration? Because they look "perfectly normal" to their parents, and that is a huge problem. A child of normal weight often looks out of place in a class of twenty-five kids, as they are one of only a few kids of normal weight.

The misguided parental perception creates a big problem for us clinicians, as generally we are met with major denial on the parents' parts and a refusal to accept what we are saying. I have had a few parents disagree with me to the point that they demand a copy of the growth chart and say they will go to the CDC or call the AAP to dispute the way the charts are made. (I gladly give them a copy of the chart after I've tried my best with counseling and education.)

Our bodies were not created for overeating. We *over*estimate how much we, and our children, need to eat to survive. We start overeating from an early age because of the influences around us. Our bodies get used to it, and so when we realize it is time to lose weight, it is difficult to reset our brains back to the correct portions. We must consciously start to notice when we are full, at which point we should stop eating. As soon as we feel that initial satisfaction of feeling full, we must train ourselves to *stop and save the rest for later or for another day.* If we start to practice this, over time we will come to know exactly the portion size we need to consume to nourish our bodies.

Another way to make sure not to overeat is to eat small, healthy portions all throughout the day. Be prepared with healthy snacks in a bag: for example, an apple, a few baby carrots, a few nuts (six almonds), or a small piece of dark chocolate. These are crunchy foods, and the more the crunch, the better the satisfaction.

- **INCORRECT FOOD CHOICES**

Then there's all the unhealthy foods adults are feeding children. We research other aspects of life, such as information needed for work projects or to pass exams, but many of us are not willing to study nutritional information about the foods we are continually putting into our bodies. Why not? *If we do not advocate for ourselves when it comes to what we put into our bodies, how can we possibly live a healthy life?*

To get you and your family on the right nutritional track, start by doing a complete, informed cleaning out of the pantry and refrigerator; there's no point in stocking our homes with the very foods that tempt our weaknesses and are not good for us, right? So cleaning out the pantry of those items is a great idea. Why stock the pantry with cookies, cakes, all types of bread, high-sugar drinks, and so on if you know you or your kids do not have the willpower to resist them? For me, I love cake; it is my food weakness. So you will never see a whole cake in my home. I buy just a slice to enjoy from time to time, and that's it.

Also, plan out meals in advance, and as you do, be familiar with both the caloric and the nutritional values. Doing so is not obsessive; you are being an advocate for you and your family's health!

• WHAT WE DRINK

Many of us drink our calories! We need a BIG mindset change, as liquids are the most dangerous contributor to excessive weight gain! We are often unaware of the amount of calories we are consuming through all the sugary and high-calorie drinks. We focus on the foods we eat and forget that we just downed four glasses of soda with our last meal! Or what about that supersized milkshake, high-calorie flavored coffee, sugar-laden iced tea, or excessive alcohol? We must become more aware of all the calories we are drinking.

Water is the best drink. Drink several cups of water throughout the day, starting first thing in the morning and ending with a drink of water right before bedtime. Let us start training our children from infancy to enjoy and drink water (pure water, that is, and not sweetened or flavored water). Children can be easily trained from very early on to cultivate good eating and drinking habits.

• PHYSICAL ACTIVITY

Our bodies were designed for movement, hence our joints being placed exactly where they are and the specific body structure with which God has blessed us. *If* we were not designed to move every day, I strongly doubt that God would have thrown in all these joints to enable our bodies to move and bend in so many fantastic, flexible ways!

Moving every day is not a choice. It is a *necessity.* I advocate that we embark on effective cardiovascular, muscle-strengthening, and stretching routines. (All three components are essential for an effective exercise routine.)

Start off slowly and in a modest way—perhaps exercising three to four times a week and then building up on that. Look for, and actively seek out, the exercise(s) you enjoy, and consistently do those. If you do not enjoy going to the gym or running, for example, do not force yourself to do them. Choose something else entirely, like the simple and worthwhile activity of walking. Make your way outside dressed in appropriate clothing for the weather and in good walking shoes, and then walk three to five miles a few days a week, and build up from there. Or buy a couple of dumbbells for home use (start out with a low weight!), then look online for effective muscle-strengthening exercises and do them a few days each week. While you're online, search for effective stretching moves you can incorporate daily.

Friends, my advice here is simple, straightforward—and inexpensive! You can do all this on your own, or look for like-minded friends or family who will join in with you and make your new exercise routine even more enjoyable and sustainable.

- **SLEEP**

What are we going to do about all the chronic insomnia that has become so prevalent in our society? It is amazing to see how many of us middle agers are not sleeping. What is on our minds keeping us up and restless? Why can't we unwind?

Maybe if we started journaling more, spending more time nourishing our spiritual and physical lives, letting go of bad relationships and letting in ones that are good, manifesting our God-given gifts to magnificence regardless of our ages and becoming great influencers, and living by the fruit of the spirit, we would all sleep well at night and get rid of sleeping pills once and for all.

In fact, I promise you will sleep better if you read this book over and over, highlight all the areas that you have to work on, and then step up and start working on them!

I also could tell you that in order to sleep better you could…get a better mattress, dim your lights, turn off the TV, put away all devices an hour before bedtime (at least), take a cool, relaxing shower, and practice deep breathing. All these do work as well, of course, but they are only *temporary fixes.*

If you do not take charge, ignite that power within you to change your life, and make key changes, you will continue to stay up at night with your mind racing at about one hundred miles an hour. Well, you cannot sleep peacefully with your mind running around like that!

You must make changes. It is the only way. (Face the problem; fix the problem!)

- **SELF-ESTEEM**

If you do not love yourself intensely, care for yourself unconditionally, adore yourself lavishly, cheer yourself on unfailingly, forgive yourself completely, and believe in yourself firmly and heartily no one else will.

Your spouse cannot. Your friends cannot. Your boss and coworkers cannot. Neither can your coaches, mentors, and teammates. And guess what? Neither can your parents once you become an adult.

Remember that you are alone while flanked by your lines. So *you* must work on *you*. No one else can. The faster you realize this, the faster your life will change for good.

With regard to weight and body-image issues, if being overweight or obese is causing a drop in your self-esteem and you can no longer hold your head up high, or you are being defensive or putting others down because of a deep-seated unhappiness about your weight—it is time to take charge, be true to yourself, and balance your life in all aspects to be able to hold your head up high again.

To me it doesn't matter what weight you precisely are, and I am also not suggesting your confidence will come back just because you might drop down to a size zero or two. What I am saying is this: If you are obviously overweight, and in the secret part of your soul you are hurting and crying yourself to sleep every night and not actively doing anything about your weight, your life will spiral out of control, and you may just keep piling on the pounds. But…*there is the power within you to take charge.* Many have done it, and you are no different.

If your weight is appropriate for your height, you have no physical symptoms or ailments, and you are confident with your body size, shape, and form, *then own it!* However, if you would like to get to a healthier weight, and if that would boost your confidence, then do so. But do not allow yourself to get obsessed with a quest for thinness. The priority and focus should be on being healthy and confident in terms of the way your body looks.

I would, however, like to emphasize that if you are overweight and obese, and it is creating sadness, restlessness, and insomnia, and also causing you to envy your friends or to be unnecessarily on the defensive, *it is time to stop the lies.* Do not act like you are "cool" with your weight and body if you are not…and then go on to criticize people who are taking charge of their weight by being proactive. *Own the fact that you do need to, and want to, lose weight, and start making changes today. Activate that power in you today…and watch yourself being transformed for good!*

I also would like to discuss your relationship with weight scales here. Yes, so many of us are fearful of weighing ourselves. Another way to describe this…*we want to live in denial. Pure denial. We are not ready to face the problem and start to fix it, so we attempt to avoid seeing the number.*

If we don't see the number, we can pretend our weight is fine and not have to deal with the problem. We can keep on lying to ourselves, even though our clothes are getting snugger or we have to start buying larger-size clothes. Well, if you do this, you are simply wasting time and procrastinating. Break free and have peace, as you will have to face this issue one day.

Why deny yourself the solution when the power lies within you to face it and fix it? Having a scale at home and weighing yourself every morning is not obsessive; it is proactive. Everyone I know who has been able to maintain a healthy weight that they are confident about weighs themselves daily. I do too. It helps me keep my weight within +/- five pounds of the healthy weight I have chosen for myself. This weight helps me walk with confidence, stand tall, and feel good in my clothes. It makes me feel well, healthy, and able to work out and exercise effectively.

As part of my morning routine, I step on my scale in the bathroom as soon as I dry myself after my shower. Guess what? *I do the same when on vacation!* The first thing I look for in the hotel bathroom is a scale. I am my own biggest advocate, and I do what it takes to keep my confidence, happiness, and health stable. I do not want to end up ten pounds heavier after a two-week vacation and then have to spend six months trying to lose the excess weight! That would be foolish.

People who dismiss others who weigh themselves daily as "obsessive" and "vain" need to refrain from thinking and acting this way. This is especially true if they are being critical of others who have what they may be looking for (in this case, a healthy body image). Too many people automatically act like this… Is it any surprise they themselves never end up getting what they want?

Humble yourselves, learn from others who have been successful with whatever you are seeking, and allow them to influence you. Being critical and holding on to jealousy in your heart, further pulls you away from your peace process!

You want peace? You want to be permanently happy? Then use the God-given power lying dormant within you to get yourself up, be influenced by all the great influencers around you, and change your life for good. You already know by the way your clothes fit whether you need to lose weight…so why not see something even more tangible, like your actual weight, to inspire you to take more action? If you want to successfully lose weight and keep it off, get a scale today and stop being fearful of what it shows you!

An Obsession with Thinness

Now, I can't move on from the self-esteem section without also discussing the other end of the spectrum: *an obsession among women with thinness, as this could lead to anorexia or bulimia.*

There seems to be an epidemic of desire to be thin, especially in some middle-aged women. The problem exists in all age groups, but it is prevalent in middle-aged women. This is obviously a psychological problem, which I believe stems from a desire to stay youthful and childlike and then starts to spiral out of control. *Neither extreme—being overweight or underweight—is healthy.* Obesity and extreme low weight are both unhealthy and can lead to your demise. So we must be careful about letting ourselves get too obsessed with keeping eternal youthful and childlike physiques.

Why would you want to look like you are twelve if you are forty-eight? Trust me—it is not attractive, and other people do not think so either (just in case you think they do). *Stop this misguided obsession before it gets to the point where you will need ongoing professional help. This problem is real and quickly gets out of control...and then you start to perceive yourself as overweight even if you are a size two, four, or even a zero!* All you want to do is just get thinner.

Please get professional help immediately if you start to notice you cannot help thinking you need to lose more and more weight even though people are telling you that you are getting too thin.

For the friends of people who are losing weight incessantly like this—please help your friends get professional help if you see this happening.

An Obsession with Plastic Surgery

A final self-esteem issue I would like to bring up is also connected to body image: we cannot talk about our physical lives and self-esteem without discussing the current obsession with plastic surgery. Why go under the knife if you can be beautiful inside and out by just nourishing your spiritual and physical lifelines? No surgical procedure will help you fix a problem that lies deep within your soul! So if you have deep-seated self-esteem issues and you try to use some kind of plastic surgery to fix your perception of yourself, that will only fix it *temporarily*. What will happen sooner or later is you will return for another procedure to see if maybe that one will give you the permanent happiness and confidence you seek. This temporary fix is the very reason people become so obsessed with having procedure after procedure after procedure (think "The Tiger Lady"!).

Stop wasting your time on temporary fixes! There are too many deformed faces out there of middle-aged women who have deep-seated heart and soul issues but who keep going around in circles having one plastic surgery after another, all in the hopes the next surgery will "heal them" and make them happy—well, it just never happens! Ladies, you were a lot prettier before the ten procedures you've had. I know your inner circle of friends cannot or won't tell you, but I am telling you now, respectfully, that you have deformed your face or disfigured your buttocks or nose—and your body just doesn't look quite so good anymore.

There is a much better option than plastic surgery! Spiritual awareness, or connecting with your spirit, will smooth out your wrinkles, keep you eternally youthful, and also make you beautiful on the inside. Nothing smooths out skin better than a healthy life-spirit connection! Add a healthy diet and regular exercise to this, and voila: gorgeous body and heart! *Done.* That's all you need.

The Desire for a Certain Body Type

Ladies, I know we all believe different types of men like some different body parts. We believe some like big buttocks, big breasts, thinness, robustness, or petite stature, and we try to transform our bodies into what we believe will attract these men.

This is a huge mistake. Your goal for transforming yourself should be for your own confidence, inner and outer beauty, and health maintenance. You should want to look in the mirror and feel good about yourself, not to check if you will be attractive to a certain male demographic. If you are trying to have a certain body type to attract or keep a certain kind of man, it's a waste of your time! And you know we cannot and should not waste precious time (see page 122)!

Choose to work on being a wholesome woman in every way who loves herself intensely. Eat right; exercise regularly; sleep well; get rid of the sleeping pills, excessive alcohol use, and/or substance abuse; and pursue your passion in life by using your God-given gifts to magnificence and connecting with your spirit daily. Do this all *for you*—then watch as the right man comes along who just wants to be part of this wholesome woman's life.

Take care of you *for you*, and you will attract a solid man, not the insecure, superficial man who is looking for big boobs, full lips, a size zero, or ginormous buttocks. *Stop attracting the wrong men into your life. Stop keeping the wrong men in your life.* These types of men need help too and have deep-seated insecurity issues. What a disaster it is when insecure meets insecure; no chance for survival for this relationship!

A man who does not understand that you are intensely beautiful as you are—your aging self, at a healthy weight and size, with a few appropriate lines on a gorgeous face that comes from a healthy diet and calm spirit, who has firm, nicely shaped buttocks from exercising; well-toned arms from weight training; a tight core from plank poses; droopy boobs (really, who cares? That's what push-up bras are for!); a radiant, confident, bright, optimistic personality from spiritual awareness; and a strong sense of self—*certainly does not deserve you. Do not settle for that type of guy.* Do not continue wasting your life away with such an insecure man. A guy who appreciates substance in a woman will come along soon to sweep you up in his arms and never let you go. Besides, you have a new goal: take care of yourself for you, not for any man.

Relinquish the "Age Excuse"

We must let go of all the excuses that are holding us back from taking charge of our lives. If you keep grasping on to excuses and false beliefs, you'll never be able to reach or maintain your weight-loss goals.

So…you are not obese because you are over forty and the fat just "sticks more" with age. Too many women over age forty (or maybe past thirty-five) let themselves go by overeating and being inactive, and then they use age as the easiest excuse. Let's drop the "age excuse!"

Forty-year-olds and above, you are overweight because you are eating too much or eating the wrong foods, not being physically active, and maybe not sleeping well. Also, you are not obese or overweight because "that's how everyone in your family is, and you are just like them." Or "I have heavy bones" is also not the reason.

Excuses and denial are a major deterrent to achieving any goals in life, including weight goals. When we face the problem, we can fix the problem.

Precious Possessions

Let us remember once again: we are spiritual beings. Your main essence is the spirit living in you. Without your spirit, you are nothing. Your spirit is your direct connection with the spiritual, heavenly realm.

But also…our physical bodies are there to house and protect our spirits. As our physical bodies are important vessels to transport our spirits around, we must equally take good care of both the spirit and the physical. Let's start doing that today—minus plastic surgery and body-type obsessions.

We all have the power to take charge and make essential changes in our lives. Let us simultaneously nourish and take care of our physical and spiritual lifelines so we can get back to smooth sailing…as we pursue permanent happiness/peace!

Chapter 8

Light and Darkness

Light always drives out darkness.

A candle burning bright in a dark room is the focus in that room.

The moon lighting the dark sky at night is the focus.

I must confess something. This chapter was not an easy one to put together, and I had to carefully connect with my spirit to get the right words.

Let us try to break it down together… Why are there natural disasters in life—earthquakes, hurricanes, and tornadoes? Why do seemingly healthy people get cancer; why do innocent kids get cancer? Why is there evil in the world? Why do some people walk around with resentment and negative energy all throughout their lives? Why are there murderers and terrorists? Why is there war between different groups of people and countries? Why is there child prostitution and sex trafficking? Why do children die of hunger? Why did 9/11 happen? Why do other unfortunate events based on human division occur?

There is darkness in our world. Anything that undermines our peace, and is contrary to the fruit of the spirit, is darkness. We are in control of some situations leading to darkness…and we are not in control of others. There are many illnesses we can prevent by working on our spiritual and physical lines, and there are some we do not have control over. We know, for example, some of the causes of cancer: smoking, obesity, excessive alcohol, environmental toxins, some infections, and possibly stress. Stress and worry are poison to us, and so I strongly believe stress has a part to play in cancer.

Stress and worry reduce our immunities and cause inflammation in our bodies, which are the precursors to malignant change. So again, we can do *all we can* to take good care of our lifelines and prevent some diseases—but some are just beyond our control. We definitely cannot control natural disasters. As for other tragedies like car accidents, we can reduce accident rates by driving safely, avoiding distractions like not texting while driving, and obeying the speed limit. We must do all we can to minimize our risks. But…*once we have done all this, and disaster still strikes, what do we do? How do we handle such situations? How do we recover from them?*

Light always drives out darkness.

A candle burning bright in a dark room is the focus in that room.

The moon lighting the dark sky at night is the focus.

How do we bring light back into our dark times and find our focus to help us move forward again?

Pure Prayer

I am a firm believer in prayer. Prayer works. *Prayer* is *asking our heavenly Creator for what we want, and believing in our hearts that He hears us and that we are healed.* If you do not believe, it will not work. You must approach God with a pure heart and strong faith. And the help of your spiritual leader—pastor, rabbi, imam, and leaders in other faiths—will help too.

However, there is nothing like personal prayer that you carry out yourself. Read your holy book, and reflect and believe in the promises for healing that you will find within its pages. Do this in a quiet, peaceful, clean, uncluttered area of your home.

I believe it helps if everything is light in this space: white sheets and comforter if there is a bed in the room; a white candle that you light (reminder—please use candles with caution); and white clothes as your attire, if possible. The point here is that *light drives out darkness*.

Don't pray in a cluttered room with black or red furniture and stuff scattered everywhere. Such surroundings do not help to quiet your spirit as much as an uncluttered, light, and airy room. This helps you connect your spirit better with God as you pray; that is my personal belief. Regardless, though, *God does hear us from anywhere, as long as we believe.*

Read the healing promises in your holy book, and affirm them. Close your eyes, quiet your spirit, remove all the negative thoughts in your soul that are flying back and forth, and visualize you or your loved one healed or freed from whatever negative situations or circumstances about which you pray. Ask God to remove all the negative energy and permanently replace it with positive energy. Talk to God like He is the best friend you have ever had. (He is.) He is right there beside you as you talk to Him, so tell Him you believe in His promises. Prayer has worked for centuries, and it still works.

No Matter the Darkness

Prepare yourself too for the dark, adverse times that are sure to come. I am sure you already have experienced some form of darkness in your life—some tragedy you were not expecting. There may be more like this to come; you just never know. But if you are prepared for it—just like with anything else in life—you will be able to recover more easily and still have hope. So if you have peace in your soul, and you are continuously pursuing peace—*that state of permanent happiness we've discussed*—you will know how to always find the light in any dark circumstance, no matter the situation.

Before we proceed, I would like to explain my understanding of spirit, soul, and physical body. Our spirits are our innermost part— our cores, our nuclei. Our souls comprise our different emotions— sadness, happiness, joy, worry, anger, peace, envy, and so on. Then our bodies are on the outside. These three components (spirit, soul, and body) need each other for us to function optimally. A soul that has mostly negative emotions will weaken the spirit and could block your connection with God. On the contrary, a soul with positive emotions strengthens your spirit and facilitates your connection with God.

Darkness and tragedy of any sort are difficult on your soul, but if your spirit is ready and you already know how to connect with God through your spirit—through awareness that arises from already being in the process of pursuing peace before tragedy strikes—you will handle dark times so much better and not be devastated. You will have the assurance and confidence that even though the situation going on may start to eat away at your physical body, and sometimes your soul and mind too, *your spirit stays intact.*

There is no illness or tragedy that can affect your spirit if you have been nourishing it and have practiced connecting to your heavenly Creator over time. It stays intact and strong despite the unforeseen negative circumstance(s).

Your life-spirit connection will give you hope, no matter what your dark situations are. If that cancer ravages your body, flesh, soul, and mind, your spirit will still live on, in life and in death. If it is a loved one going through an illness or disease, you are assured of the same for her or him. If that car accident left you paralyzed, it only touched your body; your spirit lives on. If that hurricane or tornado swept you away, your flesh and soul are gone, but your spirit lives. The loved ones you've left behind will derive hope from the assurance that you are still beside them in the spiritual heavenly realm. If Alzheimer's or mental illness affects you or your loved one, it is only affecting the mind and soul (sometimes the flesh), but not the spirit. The person may not recognize you in the physical world anymore due to their condition, but you are still connected in spirit. If you lose a loved one to a senseless shooting, their body, soul, and mind are gone, but their spirit is still connected with yours.

Without Fear of Death

Tragedy and illness can lead to death, in which our bodies and souls are removed from the physical world, but our spirits live on in the spiritual realm. We must fully understand this, so let's reflect on it and allow it to seep into our minds for good, because it is the truth.

If we carefully reflect on it, this will allow us to stop being scared of dying or death. Death is inevitable, so there is no reason to be scared of it. We all know we will not be here forever in the physical state.

When I saw visions of my dad and my sister, I saw them in their physically young states. My dad looked like he was in his forties or early fifties, as his face was plump and wrinkle-free. He was standing upright without his cane and dressed in the safari suit that he used to wear when he was young. My sister's image came from when we were younger; she was probably in her late twenties, as the dress she was wearing came from that time. She was looking healthy and pretty and did not have the ravaged, bony body she had the week before she died of cancer. Both my dad and my sister had huge smiles on their faces. This assures me that despite their bodies being traumatized by old age and cancer (respectively), their spirits were not touched by their illnesses and were being housed, after their physical deaths, in youthful bodies in the spiritual realm.

I believe their spiritual bodies will remain youthful forever. Both my father and my sister lived out their purposes on this earth—they were great influencers in their own ways—and so their influences and spirits live on.

Real Urgency

Now you realize death is nothing to be scared of, so let me tell you what we should be scared of, and about which there is real urgency: *TIME.* Not illness, dying, tragedy, or death.

Since death is inevitable, *why are we wasting time delaying fulfilling our purposes in this world?* We are all born with God-given gifts, positive instruments to be used for magnificence in our lives and other people's lives. The magnificence and impact of these gifts are meant to live on and keep influencing others even when our bodies and souls are gone from this world. *We were born to be great influencers.*

If illness or tragedy strikes today, can you comfortably say you have recognized your gifts? Have you used them to magnificence in your life? Have they influenced you and others around you positively? Would you be proud and content if the influence from those gifts lived on in this world long after your body and soul are no longer here? Would you be satisfied with the legacy of your spirit? Do you have any other gifts you need to be working on now to enable you to be an even greater influencer?

We should be scared of wasting time, not scared of dying or death. Besides, it is pointless to be procrastinating about using your God-given gifts and filling yourself instead with fear, hopelessness, and lethargy. *Be bold, courageous, fearless, and hopeful. Step out in faith, and own your gifts and your greatness.* But be aware...*you do not have forever to start to work on them!* The present is quickly becoming the past, and you are having less of a future with each passing moment. **What is the point of dying without living first?**

If you are truly living and flourishing on a daily basis, and influencing your children and loved ones on how to live and flourish, you will not be scared of death or dying.

Even if illness or disability has struck you, if your soul and spirit are still intact, you can still be a great influencer. Simply ponder, what, in your current state of illness, you can do to influence others positively. Your body may not be as whole, but as long as you have breath, your soul is still alive, as is your spirit of course—and you can still make a big change in the world.

Peace over and above Illness

Illness is a form of darkness, but there is still light in the story of every person suffering from any kind of illness, whether acute or chronic illness, temporary or terminal. Have you ever wondered how some sick people can be the happiest and most peaceful people in the world? This is because they are pursuing peace over and above their illnesses. They live by the fruit of the spirit despite their illnesses and are lights unto others.

Some of the most inspiring and influential people in the world are those who have struggled with, or are struggling with, various forms of illness or tragedy and are now using that darkness they are battling, or have battled, for the good of others. There is nothing more inspiring than seeing a person fighting a chronic illness who still lights up the world with a huge smile on their face and with hope in their heart. If they can be smiling, hopeful, and still spreading influence, no one else has an excuse for not influencing others! For what really matters in life is how we live our lives with the time granted to us, how we impact others positively, and how we continuously pursue peace in sickness and in health.

Yes, you can be struggling with, and fighting, a form of darkness (e.g., sickness or depression), but you can also make the choice to pursue peace and still be a great influencer. Illness can ravage your body and soul, while your spirit remains alive and vital. You can still make a big change in the world because your spirit is still intact. This is such a powerful truth, and my hope is that everyone reading this book and suffering from a chronic illness can understand that his or her gifts are still needed *and are still here* in the world. It certainly takes a lot more effort, courage, and strength while in the state of darkness to pursue peace and use your positive instruments for good, but the impact and the rewards are multiplied.

Everywhere there is darkness, there is a light waiting to shine through. You can change the world in two days, two years, or ten years. It is not the amount of time you have but the impact you make and the lives that are changed for good through your influence. So start using your time wisely, with peace and influence, right now.

The Damage of Darkness

Let's consider other types of darkness in the world: hatred, violence, racism and other human divisions, jealousy, fits of rage, drunkenness, drug addictions, idolatry, witchcraft, orgies, selfish ambition, sexual immorality, and chronic worry. I have never seen a person with envy in their heart, hardheartedness, a lack of forgiveness, and antipathy toward others—a person who curses his brother, holds up negative energy against his neighbor, or taps into the dark principalities of this world—ever find peace.

Darkness without any light is bad news. It is in contrast to pursuing peace. (And can't we just see it—literally? The darkness shows up all around such a person in the form of their outward appearance, their health, their lack of contentment, their lack of personal growth, the blockages of blessings from God, and their inability to ever find their life purpose.)

Unfortunately, if such people do not let go of the darkness, it trickles down from generation to generation—from child to child; into and through extended family units; and, insidiously, into communities and the world at large. More importantly and more seriously, it can be transmitted from generation to generation spiritually.

If their spirit is continuously filled with negative energy and emotions, the person is destroying the very nucleus of their body and their connection with God. They are of no use to themselves or to anyone around them. They are moving darkness around, spreading negative energy around, and making life difficult and nonexistent for themselves and others.

Such a plethora of dark acts can make life so difficult for the rest of us as well. *How do we move away from these acts and completely set ourselves free from them?*

Ask God for a discerning spirit to identify these people holding on to darkness, as sometimes they disguise themselves with a seemingly friendly attitude…but their spirits are in contrast to the fronts that they put forward. It is important to recognize these types of people so that we can distance ourselves from them. Otherwise, their negative energy will eventually permeate our souls and spirits too!

Energies—both positive and negative—in the spiritual realm are strong. Do not allow negative energy around you to poison your soul and spirit. Remember to ask God daily to only bring positive people and energies around you.

Dark Acts of the Flesh

I would like to discuss a few of these acts of the flesh:

- **CONSTANT WORRY**

Worry is such a common problem that I want to do my best to help us realize the harm it is doing in our lives. Please know though I'm not referring to the *occasional* worry/worries. It is *constant* worry that is a form of darkness because it undermines our processes of pursuing peace and separates us from the fruit of the spirit. *Where there is worry, faith is missing.* Worry and faith are in opposition to one another.

Short-lived worry is healthy and a normal human behavior. So it is okay to worry about your kids' well-being, about whether that job interview will have a good outcome, and whether you'll end up getting good grades. These are normal thought processes in order to be successful at our goals. However, *constant worry* is a major deterrent to pursuing peace.

Constant worry is essentially when we are thinking and juggling the same thoughts, life decisions, or problems over and over in our minds without clear solutions or plans to turn them around. It is also when we allow fear to prevent us from taking action.

If you are constantly worrying about a problem that you have the power to change, you must grab that power and change. If it is beyond your inner power and your control, you simply must let it go.

We must all let go of constant worrying. It is darkness, and it will continue to hinder us from "doing." Let us all stop worrying—and instead, start doing.

- **JEALOUSY**

I'm also not referring to the *occasional* streaks of jealousy. It is perfectly fine to look at a person whom you would like to be like and have a quick jealous thought about their talent or skill set before you start to hope that you can one day achieve what they've achieved— and you simply hold only positive thoughts about them after that. Not negative thoughts, but curious and wishful thoughts that help you put your plans, hopes, and dreams into forward motion in a positive way so that hopefully one day you can be at the greatness they are at. (This kind of quick-lived jealousy is more of a form of admiration than anything else.)

However, *deep-seated jealousy,* wherein you are constantly envying others' successes and achievements, gossiping about them, and trying to spoil their reputations or hindering them in any way, is a dark attitude—and you must let go of it!

If you indulge in deep-seated jealousy and chronic worry, it will block your spirit connection with God, and you will never be able to achieve your goals and live a meaningful life.

- **FAVORITES**

God has no favorites, contrary to what most of us believe.

As humans, many of us think, hope, and believe He does. Many of us have been reared and taught by others that He does! So we fill our hearts with this false belief and walk around feeling sorry for, dismissive of, or even angry at, people we do not deem to be God's "favorites." In some situations, we do not want to have anything to do with them; in extreme cases, we want those individuals or groups of individuals wiped off the face of the earth (think Hitler and the Jews and other forms of religious extremism, which we are experiencing all too often in our current world).

Well, God loves the person we label an "atheist" equally as much he loves the person we label a "Christian," a "Jew," or a "Muslim," and so on and so on.

I am very sure many reading this right now completely disagree with me: "How can God love the atheist the same way He loves me? I go to church every Sunday, and sometimes even on Wednesdays to attend the midweek service! I pay my tithes. I have told God I love Him, and I sing praises to Him. The atheist does not believe in God. How can God love him the same exact way He loves me?" I know it is really tough to read this, but *God loves everyone the same exact way as He loves you.*

God loves all His creation the same, and He wants a limitless, joyful life for all of us. God loves what is in our hearts and deepest souls; it's not about what we say, believe, look like, or even pretend to be on the outside. *God has His eyes on you and is seeking your attention as much as He has eyes on the atheist and is seeking their attention too.* He will never give up on anyone. He understands none of us will ever be perfect, no matter how hard we try. He knows full well the Christian will never be perfect…and neither will the agnostic, the Muslim, or atheist.

Why would God create us all in His image…and then have favorites? It is like the situation with parents and their child. A child may not want anything to do with the parents, but good, loving, responsible, and wise parents will love their child unconditionally despite this. Why? Because loving parents love their children dearly and unconditionally. Love transcends all.

So my apologies if I offended or disappointed anyone with the simple truth that God loves us all equally. But it is truth.

- **LABELING**

The creator of the universe is seeking the content of our hearts. This means He does not care about the labels we place on each another. Religious labels, professional labels, political labels, and economic labels mean nothing to our Creator. Only the content of our hearts mean something and everything to Him.

Have you met someone who has labeled himself an agnostic or atheist but is living by all the fruit of the spirit? And have you met a person who is labeled Christian and not living by any of the fruit of the spirit? I have. *Case in point: Labels don't matter. What's inside matters.*

Christian, Muslim, Hindu, Jew… There are other labels I would like to get rid of too: the labels of our professions. Have you ever thought for one second that professional/work labels are unnecessary too?

Ponder this: My profession is only what I do to make a living, have a roof over my head, earn my daily bread, enjoy a bed to sleep in, give my kids a good education, and afford to travel. First and foremost, I am a human being seeking to interact with people—all people, *not only specific groups*—so as to leave a positive mark wherever I've been. I have no aspiration to be perfect, but I do have a goal to continually seek the meaning of life, and that is why I am sharing my convictions with you in the form of a book.

A high-level executive, an attorney, an engineer, a physician, a plumber, a UPS driver, a pastor, a rabbi, an imam, a hairdresser, a teacher, a stay-at-home parent, a small-business owner, and a sports coach are all human beings on different economic levels, but they do have things in common: (1) They all need provisions to keep their families safe and to provide shelter, food, education, healthcare, and so on, and (2) most importantly, they are all seeking the meaning of life—whether this be consciously or subconsciously. They all have a powerful spiritual essence and are all on a spiritual path. (How's that for unifying different and diverse classes of people?)

Let's stop casting labels and being divisive when it comes to other people. It isn't morally right. And it isn't part of God's plan either. *This one conscious act on our parts, where we start seeking people's hearts and souls instead of focusing on their labels—will make a BIG impact on our quest for world peace, world unity, and eventual acceptance and love of all people.*

Another Time

As for the other physical acts of the flesh that plague our world and societies today, including violence, racism, and other forms of human divisions, let me simply state that the motivation behind such dark acts is such a huge and phenomenally intricate topic that I am going to choose to discuss this at a later time. I hope we can meet again soon to learn and continue to grow together regarding this.

And of course, the acts I've just mentioned are in contrast to the fruit of the spirit and completely separate the people who commit them from the process of pursuing peace. The fruit of the spirit are perfect light—and perfect light drives out darkness.

Time for Perfect Light!

Make a change today. Renew your mind, soul, and spirit. Let go of all the negativity, and change your character and your inside by choosing to live by the fruit of the spirit, and get back on the pursuit of peace/permanent happiness. This is "the only way" your life can have real meaning.

Chapter 9

Ask for Help

To succeed in all aspects of our lives, we need help from others.

According to the famous saying, "It takes a village to raise a child." However, it also takes a village to raise an adult. The moment we realize we cannot do it all by ourselves, we will completely transform our lives! We all need coaches, mentors, advisors, influencers, encouragers, nannies, babysitters, personal assistants, handymen…and sometimes even Uber drivers to make our lives work!

Many adults will help us for free, if only we ask. Some we do have to pay for of course, since it may be what they do for a living.

It's Good Business

Help is necessary to succeed in all aspects of our lives. You have already read about the people who have helped me live out my personal life effectively, and I thank them right now, as I would not be who I am today without them. But the same applies if you own a business or are thinking of owning one: *you cannot, and you should not, do everything by yourself! If you do, your business will not grow.*

If you are trying to cut expenses or to keep all the profits for yourself by "doing it all," you are limiting your professional and entrepreneurial success. It is okay to start off in the early stages doing most aspects by yourself, or with a lean staff, but you must add good, hard-to-replace staff as time goes on. Do not be fearful of doing so. If you are stretched thin and chronically drained by running around doing everything and your business is not growing or making a profit, it is time to add good staff. Do not worry about being able to pay them, and other such fears you may have. You will be able to cover payroll if you believe in yourself and have some talent around you supporting you. So allow others to bring their gifts, talents, and ideas to help you and your business soar.

You must, however, be wise in terms of whom you hire, as the employees you choose can make or break you. Look for coaches and mentors in the field of your business to help guide you as to whom to choose to join your team. You will also learn about this as you go.

In the beginning years of my practice, I hired many easy-to-replace staff; this drained me and limited the growth of my practice. After three or four years, I realized the traits and qualities to look for in hiring staff, and this knowledge helped me surround myself with hard-to-replace people who are dedicated to their personal successes as well as the success of their jobs, and my practice has benefited greatly from them.

Be sure to keep all your senses acute and fully activated when on the job. Remember to not only consider the "obvious" choices—those people close to you or who you feel are similar to you—to be mentors but to break away from the stereotypical type and stretch your asking hand out far away from your circle. You will be surprised who will be willing to help!

This was true for my business: the key person who helped me with all the questions I had about opening my medical practice was someone I initially did not consider a likely candidate!

How do you find someone from outside your circle to coach you in your endeavors? Go to networking events, read books, do some online research, and simply ask for referrals from others. There is help all around you, so do not be discouraged. *Reach out, persist, and you will find help for every goal you want to reach in your life.*

As I write this book, I am putting my God-given gifts, talents, and life experiences into it. But that's not all: I have also researched online about finding an editor for my manuscript; getting a good agent; and determining my options for publishing. I also scheduled myself for two writing conferences, in February and May, to meet potential agents.

No one can be successful without seeking out help. Work hard, and then allow others to help you with achieving your goals.

Chapter 10

What We Need to Live Will Follow

Nourishing our spiritual and physical lifelines makes us rich in heart and soul issues, which is the only kind of riches we need to survive and thrive.

Money and materialism are not needed for true soul survival; we first must fight for the survival of our souls.

Every poor man would like to tell the rich man how lucky he is to have all that money. Every rich wise man would like to tell the poor man that money does not buy happiness—that it may buy him a more comfortable sofa to sit on, but it cannot purchase joy and peace.

Readers, please notice I included the word *wise* in the previous sentence, as only the rich men *who are also wise* understand this. If you are rich and have not gained wisdom or maturity, you cannot understand that money won't buy joy. Many of you struggle with this choice: "Do I want money, or do I want peace? I would like both. Why can't I have both?"

First let me remind you: Achieving prosperity is not the primary reason we work. We work in order to be great influencers.

You want to positively influence others and yourself, of course. And make your work something that keeps you wanting to get up enthusiastically every morning. Get up and go to work because you love influencing and inspiring others, and you are being inspired yourself.

But here is some more good news. We can have both...with just one caveat: We can only acquire meaningful money, wealth, and riches if we are living by the fruit of the spirit and continuously pursuing peace. If your focus in life is primarily on achieving permanent happiness or peace, the money, wealth, riches, and whatever else you need to live will follow. Trust me on this.

Which Came First, the Chicken or the Egg?

The primary goal in this lifetime must be nourishing your spiritual and physical lifelines, being of good character, working hard toward your goals, being patient and resilient, and being a great influencer, encourager, inspiration, and example to others on any path you embark on. Then all you need to do is *watch* as your life comes together with the right team of people and a set of circumstances where you are making enough money to live a good life...and with peace that is all yours to keep and enjoy. So you *can* have both peace and enough riches...as long as your intentions are good and your priorities are in the right order.

You will have both money and peace, and be able to keep money and peace, until the day you depart from this earth.

Chapter 11

It Is All Possible

What is possible for you?

It is possible to live a life of permanent happiness/peace and get the most out of life. You can live a life full of meaning, and you can live out your life-given purpose. *Yes, you can live a permanently happy life, a life filled with peace.* (Remember, peace is enough, and it is the ultimate state of well-being and fulfillment. It is the state of wholesomeness. Happiness is good, but just not enough.)

We all have the God-given power within us. As we have learned through this book, there are three steps to living a meaningful and peaceful life:

- The first step is to live by the fruit of the spirit.

- The second step is to nourish our spiritual and physical lives.

- The third step is we must use our God-given gifts to inspire and elevate others, as well as ourselves. Unless we are influencing others positively, we cannot live a meaningful life.

So this is it—the three simple steps needed for that desired state: the state of *permanent happiness* and *ongoing peace* regardless of any life circumstances.

Following these steps offers the only way to pursue peace, find joy, live a meaningful life, and fulfill our life purposes. **And that, my friends, is my hope for every human being in this universe.**

Thank you for reading my book. It's been a great honor writing and sharing with you. I hope we can read and learn together again soon.

Iyabo Ojikutu, MD

May 2017

Made in the USA
Columbia, SC
27 August 2017